A SYNTHESIS OF
The Spiritual Life

A SYNTHESIS OF

The Spiritual Life

DOM WULSTAN MORK, O.S.B.

THE BRUCE PUBLISHING COMPANY
MILWAUKEE

IMPRIMI POTEST:

✠ Gerald Benkert, O.S.B., Abbot

NIHIL OBSTAT:

John A. Schulien, S.T.D.
Censor librorum

IMPRIMATUR:

✠ William E. Cousins
Archbishop of Milwaukee
January 23, 1962

Library of Congress Catalog Card Number: 62–11166
© 1962 The Bruce Publishing Company
MADE IN THE UNITED STATES OF AMERICA

Introduction

This book is to be meditated, taught, and lived. It is primarily a textbook of the spiritual life, although it can be used for spiritual reading. It will perfectly achieve its purpose only when the principles in each chapter are applied practically to daily life, when they are related to each detail of life.

The text itself is a concise but comprehensive study of the essentials of the Christian life, hence of the life of union with God. We have tried to keep subdivision to the minimum in order to avoid confusion and to attain unity. Hence, many interesting and even useful bypaths either have not been followed or else have been merely opened.

The synthesis is best expressed in the closing words of the Canon of the Mass: "Through Him and with Him and in Him is to Thee, God the Father almighty, in the unity of the Holy Spirit, all honor and glory." Our life as Christians is Trinitarian, for we have been re-created by grace in the image of the life of the Trinity, more precisely, in the image of the life of the Son. Now and in eternity we must give glory to the Father as His adopted sons. The function of the Holy Spirit in our regard is to unite us to the Incarnate Son and in Him to the Father.

There is no division of the spiritual life in this book into the three ways — the purgative, illuminative, and unitive — nor into the phases of asceticism and mysticism, not because we don't hold with these divisions, but because the aim of the book is to present the Christian life as a "unity in Trinity," glory to the Father as His adopted sons. Moreover, such divisions are confusing to beginners, who tend to think of them as stages through which one passes and then leaves, or permanently attains, instead of regarding them as overlapping, as is the case with those who have made some progress. Perhaps they would be better taught as such at a higher level of instruction.

We have not treated the religious life as an entity apart, but rather the Christian life itself, and the religious state as a professed dedication to its perfection. Hence, the vows of chastity and obedience are commitments to love; and that of poverty, to attachment to Christ. The prescriptions of Rules and Constitutions are viewed from the perspective of our Christian vocation as adopted sons, and thus, again, a unified outlook is the hoped-for result.

We have considered attachment before detachment, because the latter is only possible if one is attached to Christ, or trying to become so. If one is attached to Him, he is *ipso facto* detached from everyone and everything else.

No particular school of spirituality is favored here. Although this book in its original outline form was first prepared as conference notes for the Benedictine novice mistresses of North America and given to them at their workshop in Indianapolis in 1957, all schools of spirituality have been studied and points of similarity stressed in an "eirenic method" of seeking what the great masters of the spiritual life have to teach us about our duty of glory as adopted sons.

But we have been more concerned to know what the source of dogma, God's word, tells us of the meaning and means of the spiritual life. For this effort the contemporary biblical revival and developments in dogma have been most valuable.

This book was prepared primarily as a textbook for novices or postulants, and this end has been kept in view throughout. As such, it would be the text used by the novice master and novices in the daily conference on the principles of the spiritual life. It could be kept by the religious after profession, as a renewal of the novitiate, especially on days of recollection and the annual retreat. Another use of the book would be for the period of renewal which is the custom in some communities before perpetual vows. In its original form it has been found useful as the basis for retreat conferences, as well as for series of conferences to religious and laity.

If the book is to provide or suggest the matter for the daily class in spiritual theology in the novitiate, it could very well be considered to be a core book, with which the other classes — Scripture, Liturgy, the Rule and Constitutions — could be integrated, and thus the novice would better obtain a unified view of the whole spiritual life from the basis of dogmatic theology. There are places in the book where special matter, e.g., that pertaining to a community's spirit, work, and devotions, can easily be introduced.

The style is succinct for two reasons: to present to the religious a book that they can more conveniently keep and carry about, and to present to the novice master material for commentary rather than ready-made conferences. Therefore the matter for each conference must be prepared, and for this reason especially a reading list is appended to the book. Not only study, but meditation and prayer will be means to making the matter meaningful, living, and convincing.

A teaching procedure for novitiate classes would be to lecture on the matter in each chapter until the chapter has been finished, while, at the same time, the novices carry out privately the practices and examens in the "Individual Application" section. Several days could then be devoted to the questions and projects in the "Group Questions and Activities" section, and, last, a symposium could be held on assigned reading from other authors. The conferences are not enough. The matter must be made practical and the novice must be made to see his life in relation to the synthesis.

This book is only a suggestion. The Holy Spirit, who is the love of Father and Son, is active in the Church, forming religious into the image of Christ. Let us listen to His voice.

To the Student

There are two key words that summarize this book: *Glory* and *Son*. In fact, they summarize the whole Christian life, the religious life. They must be the key words for the novitiate. Learn them well, for the realities which they symbolize summarize our eternity.

"Let us make mankind in our own image and likeness" (Gen. 1:26). This intention of God is the secret of life — the life of God is to be ours. Christ has revealed what that life is: it is one and three, Unity and Trinity.

God has one occupation — glory to Himself. But God is one in three Persons: the life of God is glory to the Father through the Son in the unity of both who is the Holy Spirit.

Our life is in the image and likeness of God's life. The "mystery of his will" (Eph. 1:10) is that our chief occupation now and in eternity is glory to the Father through the Son in the unity of the Holy Spirit. The Father is our End, the Son, our Way, the Holy Spirit, our Means, in that His work is to form us into the image of the Son, in whom alone the Father is well pleased. The Holy Spirit is selfless, for He is Love.

Through Christ, in Him, and with Him, is all glory to the Father in the unity of the Holy Spirit.

This is the Christian life; therefore, the religious life. This is the occupation of the novitiate and of eternity already begun.

Veni, Sancte Spiritus!

Contents

A SYNTHESIS OF
The Spiritual Life

CHAPTER 1

God's Life in God

> **What I hope to achieve:** *To realize, insofar as the Holy Spirit permits, the inner life of God. To understand that my life has been re-created by grace in the image of that life, and that my chief occupation is to co-operate with the Holy Spirit in achieving that likeness to it that He wills for me.*

At the beginning of our study of the spiritual life it is necessary that we first realize God's intentions for us. In our life of love we cannot please Him if we do not clearly understand what He wants of us. "The Lord has made all things for himself,"[1] He tells us in the Book of Proverbs: insofar as we are creatures we have been created for God. We shall consider this end of creation in the next chapter. But what of our status as human beings? "Let us make mankind in our own image and likeness."[2] These words of God express His

---

[1] Prov. 16:4. (Unless otherwise indicated, all citations from the Old Testament are from the Confraternity translation [Paterson, N. J., 1952 ff.].)

[2] Gen. 1:26.

1

specific intention in creating us and the way in which we are to fulfill that intention.

God is spirit, with perfect intellect and will. In creating us in His image, He made our principal part, our soul, spirit, with intellect and will. Our body is our link with material creation, but our soul is in the likeness of God. Like Him we can know truth and will good. Like Him we can know Him as Truth and limitless, perfect Good. By our very nature as human beings we are in the image of the divine essence.

But in creating man God did not intend that he should be on the purely natural level. The Hebrew version of the above-quoted words of God in the Book of Genesis indicates that He intended to create man in the closest possible likeness to Himself. God, therefore, elevated our first parents to the supernatural level, to a plane of living similar to His own, by giving them a share in His own life. This life was sanctifying grace, which would develop, after the trial period, into the beatific vision. Our first parents failed their trial, lost for themselves and their posterity the divine life and its fulfillment. But in His love God sent His Son, made man like us, to atone for the human race, and thereby restore to it the divine life and the beatific vision.

We have been created, as human beings, in the image of the divine essence, and re-created, as Christians, in the likeness of the divine life. What is the distinction between these two facts? If our lives were to be led only on the natural level we would still be similar to God because, like Him, we would have intellect and will, and could do what God does, know and love Him. Of course, this knowledge and love would be indirect: we could only know Him through His creation and love Him only as so known. This would be relatively difficult, but we would still be able to do something Godlike, and something that no animal could do.

But in giving our first parents, and ourselves, through Christ, His own life, God gave them and us the ability to know and love Him, not grasped indirectly, but as He knows and loves Himself, as He is in Himself. He has elevated us above our nature and has given us a share in His own. We live by His life so that we can live His life. We can and must do what He does.

But what does God do? In what does His life consist? Christ has revealed the secret of God's life, and this secret is the foundation dogma of Christianity: God's life is Trinitarian. Three divine Persons possess simultaneously the one divine nature. There is in God, therefore, Unity and Trinity. We have been created, naturally, in the image of the Unity — the divine essence — and re-created, supernaturally, in the image of the Trinity, which is God's life.

But does this mean that we are to perform the functions which the three divine Persons perform within the Trinity? Again God has revealed His mind in our regard: "Out of love he predestined us for himself to become through Jesus Christ his adopted children, conformably to the good pleasure of his will, to the praise of his resplendent grace, with which he has adorned us in his beloved Son."[3]

---

[3] Eph. 1:5–6.

We are to be by adoption what the Son is by nature; forming us into the likeness of the Son is the work of the Holy Spirit. This is, briefly, how our life is to be Trinitarian. This is God's intention for us; our spiritual life, therefore our total life, has no other pattern. Because of this fact we must first attempt some understanding of the Holy Trinity — God's life in God, in which image we have been re-created as Christians.

This is the mystery of mysteries, and we can approach the Holy Trinity only with an awareness of the infinite gap between the triune God and ourselves. We can only grope toward understanding with metaphors, while waiting for the revelation of the beatific vision. But what we can understand we must, and this understanding must change our lives. The dogma of the Holy Trinity must be taken from the creeds, from the abstract, and be for us in the concrete what we profess it to be, the fundamental truth of our faith.

Christ clearly and beautifully revealed this mystery in His discourse to His Apostles and His prayer to the Father after the Last Supper (cf. Jn. 14–17). These chapters of St. John should be read slowly and prayerfully. The names of the Persons and their relations with each other are here well stated. The relations of each with us and of us with them are also indicated. We shall consider all of this in more detail when we have studied the essential fact that there are in God, in the divine nature, three Persons. Trinity in Unity.

We begin with the notion of nature, for it is the one divine nature which is common to the three Persons. Nature makes a thing what it is. For example, an

Christ not only revealed the plurality of Persons in God but also told us their names and relationships. Theology has, from Christ's revelation, attempted to give us some understanding of these relationships. We must remember that whatever theologians have written has the character of metaphor; we are, when all possible human "explanations" have been given, still in the presence of the mystery of mysteries.

We reason that the divine nature has to have intellect and will because of the form of creation. Its order of ends and means, its orderly structures and functions, argue a divine intellect to conceive and an equally divine will to execute. And because this nature is simple we also conclude that God is His intellect and will. Were God distinct from His intellect and will, the divine nature would involve plurality and imperfection.

The intellect in the Father is occupied in knowing Himself, His divine nature. Since God is simple, His thought is simple, a single idea. This thought, which comprises all His being, He expresses in a single Word. The Word is the expression of the Father and has personality. Proceeding from the Father this Person is the Son. The Father, knowing His being in the Son, and the Son, knowing His being in the Father and knowing this being as infinite good, love each other with a single love, which also has personality. The Holy Spirit is the love of Father and Son; He is the union of Father and Son.

The procession of the divine Persons, of the Son from the Father and of the Holy Spirit from both, is the life of God. Because of their relation to each other, each Person has His own "role" in the Trinity: the Father gives His being to the Son, the Son pleases the Father, and the Holy Spirit is their mutual love. The Father is the source in the Trinity, the source of being for the Son, and with Him for the Holy Spirit. The Son-made-man will say, "Whatever the Father possesses is mine."[4] The Father is source, this is His characteristic note, the supreme source of all that exists within and outside of the Trinity. Everything proceeds from Him. He is the source of the Son by way of intellectual generation. He is, with the Son, the source of the Holy Spirit by way of love. He is the creative source of all being in the universe, the very source of all the elect, predestined for the vision of His Face.[5]

Not only the existence of the Trinity but also the names of the Persons were revealed by Christ. He is the Son, because He has received His being from the Father. The essential function of a son is to please his father, and in the life of the Trinity this is the "role" of God the Son. How does He do this? First, by His very being. He is the image of the Father; all that the Father is the Son is, except His Person of Father. "The Father and I are one."[6] What greater pleasure can a father receive from his son than to see in him all of his good qualities? A son, by being the image of his father's good, fulfills his essential duty of pleasing his

---

[4] Jn. 16:15. (Unless otherwise indicated, all citations from the New Testament are from the Kleist-Lilly translation [Milwaukee: The Bruce Publishing Co., 1954].)

[5] M. Philipon, O.P., La Trinité dans Ma Vie (Paris: Editions St.-Paul, 1956), p. 17.

[6] Jn. 10:30.

father. In the Trinity the Father gives the Son His being, and the Son pleases the Father by being all that the Father is: "He who sees me sees the Father."[7] "This is my Son, the beloved, with whom I am well pleased."[8]

Second, the Son pleases the Father by His love. He knows the Father as Good, His Good, and loves Him, giving Himself totally to the Father. We can best express these two ways in which the Son pleases the Father by the word glory. We shall study glory in the next chapter and relate what we have learned to glory in the Trinity, but here it suffices to state that the Son is the glory of the Father, by His being the image of the Father and by His knowledge and love of Him. The Gloria Patri could as well be reworded: Glory to the Father in the Son in the union of the Holy Spirit.

St. John calls the Son the Word, and aptly so, for a word is the expression of a thought, a symbol manifesting a thought. The Son as a distinct Person is the expression of the single thought in the intellect of the Father, which thought is the divine Being. But especially is the Word a most fitting name for the Son since He is the revelation of God, the voice of God, speaking first in creation: "Creation then is the work of the Word of God, and that is why it is also a revelation, for when God speaks he can only utter himself."[9] Later He spoke through the law and the prophets; there

---

[7] Jn. 14:9.

[8] Mt. 3:17.

[9] M. E. Boismard, O.P., St. John's Prologue (London: Blackfriars Publications, 1957), p. 85.

is in Second Isaia an indication that this revealing
Word is the Person of the Son who pleases the Father:

> For just as from the heavens
>> the rain and snow come down
> And do not return there
>> till they have watered the earth,
>> making it fertile and fruitful,
> Giving seed to him who sows
>> and bread to him who eats,
> So shall my word be
>> that goes forth from my mouth;
> It shall not return to me void,
>> but shall do my will,
>> achieving the end for which I sent it.[10]

Lastly, as the Word made flesh, He was the incarnate
revelation of God, of God's life, and of the life of man
with Him. The application of the term Word for God-
revealing is perfect, for what is a word but the revelation of a thought?

The Holy Spirit is the love of Father and Son for
each other.[11] Receiving His being from both, He is the
bond, the union, of both. When the Father loves the
Son, and the Son the Father, they love, as it were, by
means of the Holy Spirit, for He is their love. His
"role" in the Trinity is selfless, for love is selfless.

This is the life of God. This is God's happiness: the
procession of Son and Holy Spirit, Father and Son
knowing and loving each other. What we have studied
as separate acts we must remember are all one act in

---

[10] Isa. 55:10–11.
[11] Cf. St. Thomas, *Summa Theologica*, I, q. 37, a. 1.

God. And neither is there a time sequence. God lives in the eternal now.

Because of the one divine nature all three Persons are present together; there may not be one without the other two, and each Person is entirely present in the other two. For example, in the Blessed Sacrament there is truly the Person of Christ, but also present are the Father and the Holy Spirit.

Although each Person has His distinct "role" in the Trinity, all three Persons act together outside the sphere of Trinitarian life. We ascribe or "appropriate" certain works to certain Persons, but actually the operation is common to the whole Trinity. "The action of a being is in proportion to the nature of that being. Nature is a principle of action. . . . Hence, as many natures, so many activities. In God nature is one, and accordingly activity is one."[12]

We were created as human beings in the image of the divine essence, because we have intellect and will, and we were re-created as Christians in the likeness of the Trinity, because we have a share in the divine life. We have tried to understand something of the life of God, but we have only begun. This is a lifelong meditation, not only because it is a strict mystery, but also because it is the exemplar of our life.

INDIVIDUAL PRACTICES

1. For meditation: Before the heavenly bodies and before even air existed, there was only God, the Trinity, the

---

[12] A. Janssens, *The Mystery of the Trinity* (Fresno: Academy Library Guild, 1954), p. 101.

Father begetting the Son, Father and Son knowing and loving Each Other in Their mutual love, the Holy Spirit. In this eternal activity is God's happiness.

2. Meditate on the fact that creation is completely unnecessary to God's being and happiness.

3. Meditate, on other days during which this chapter is studied, on the life of the Trinity, with no reference to self. Adore the Trinity. Praise, thank, and love God for the divine processions, for the "roles" of the three Persons.

4. Meditate on the *Gloria* of the Mass.

5. Memorize for recollection one of the gospel passages in which Christ speaks to or of the Father.

6. Say the *Our Father* with the direction to the Father which Christ gave it.

7. Use for recollection the expressions: (To Christ) You are the being of the Father. You are the image of the Father. You are the glory of the Father. (To the Holy Spirit) You are the union of Father and Son. You are the love of Father and Son. You are love in the Trinity.

GROUP QUESTIONS AND ACTIVITIES

1. Discuss *natural* and *supernatural*.

2. How would one live on the purely natural level?

3. Are Catholics in general Trinitarian or Unitarian in practice?

4. Which prayers of the Mass are addressed to God the Father?

5. Find psalms in which the Father addresses the Son, and the Son, the Father.

6. Collect the passages in St. John's Gospel in which Christ refers to the Father.
7. Make a rather complete study of the Trinity: fore-shadowing in the Old Testament; revelation in the New Testament; what the Fathers, St. Thomas, and theologians have written. This study should not be omitted.

CHAPTER 2

The Purpose of Our Life

What I hope to achieve: *To realize God's twofold purpose in creating me — glory and happiness — and to relate everything in my life to that purpose.*

When we want something we are only admitting our imperfection: We don't have everything. When God created man He didn't do so because He was lacking something. God has everything. He is unbounded perfection. He created man ". . . only to communicate His perfection, which is His goodness."[1] He gave being, a share in His goodness. Creation on God's part was a gift, a pure act of love.

We exist because of God's love, but we exist for God. "The Lord has made everything for his own ends."[2] Whatever God does, He must have Himself as His final object, because only He is unbounded Good, only He can be the fitting object of the divine will. Only God is worthy of God. He primarily loves Himself,

---

[1] St. Thomas Aquinas, *Summa Theologica*, I, q. 44, a. 4, translation of the English Dominican Fathers (New York: Benziger Brothers, Inc., 1947).
[2] Prov. 16:4.

wills Himself, therefore, because fastening His will primarily on one of His creatures would be to admit that that creature was a greater good than Himself. God, in loving His creatures, must love His perfection in them, knowing them only in reference to Himself. And creatures cannot exist for themselves but only in reference to God. God has communicated His goodness to them that they might give Him glory. His rational creatures have the ability to recognize that all of their being, all of their perfections, are from God. They have the duty to do this and to glorify God for what they recognize. Nonrational creatures glorify God by their very existence, following His natural laws.

God's primary end in creating man, then, is that man might give Him glory. We must at the beginning of the novitiate realize this as deeply as we can, because it is the solid foundation of our spiritual life. This realization will make us "theocentric," God-centered, rather than "anthropocentric," man-centered. It may save us from spiritual disaster in later years.

Glory to God, our chief duty in life, includes all our other religious obligations. St. Augustine defined glory as "clear knowledge joined to praise" (Clara cum laude notitia).[3] This definition tells us not only what glory is but also how we give it. Praise presumes that there is something to praise. Hence, glory is first of all objective, i.e., some perfection actually exists in another person, and it is this perfection we praise. In God there is all perfection. Therefore God Himself is His objective

---

[3] Contra Maximinum, in Patrologia Latina (P.L.), Vol. 42, col. 770.

glory. *Gratias agimus Tibi propter magnam gloriam Tuam.*

Glory, then, must be an act of the intellect, recognizing perfection in the other person — *formal glory.* This is the "clear knowledge" of the definition. Without this knowledge praise would be false, for it would have no true basis. The deeper the knowledge, the truer the praise, the greater the glory. Hence, the more we know God, the better will we be able to give Him glory. Note that the term here is *know,* not *know about.* A person may be quite ignorant of the byways of dogmatic theology and yet have a deep knowledge of God. While a knowledge of dogma helps, it remains just that, a knowledge of dogma. What we must pursue is a knowledge of God based on dogma, and this is essentially the work of the supernatural virtues of faith and charity and the gifts of understanding and wisdom. When we know God we know His perfections because God is perfection.

Third, glory is praise — *expressed glory.* The perfection exists in another, we know it, we tell the other about it. But our praise of God implies more than telling Him, intellectually or vocally, about Himself. Our praise includes love and service, for each of these is a means of telling God of the perfection of His being.

That the prayer of pure praise is glory to God is easy to see. But so is the prayer of adoration, for by it we tell God He is the Author of creation, of our being, that He is perfection, that we are totally dependent upon His love. The prayer of thanksgiving tells Him of His love evidenced by past and present favors; reparation praises His love for us in spite of our failure to respond. Finally, petition is reminding Him of that love which will always give us what is for our good. The prayer of the liturgy is glory, for by it we are performing all of these acts, through, with, and in Christ.

What is our love of God but telling Him that He is the only fitting object of our love, infinitely good in Himself, infinitely worthy of our constant choice? Love is the highest form of glory.

And service, proceeding from adoration, is telling God that He is our Creator, that therefore we belong totally to Him: our whole person, our interests, our time. "I have glorified you on earth by completing the work you gave me to do."[4]

Our chief duty to God, glory, translates itself each moment into prayer, love, and service. A simple act of obedience, such as washing dishes, gives God glory, for we perform it because He wills it, and He is our Creator, and the One whom we supremely love. Our action is a means of telling God these things about Himself. Thus in this small task we have the three elements of glory: *expressed*, based on *formal*, which, in turn, is based on God's *objective* glory, Himself.

In the first chapter we stated that the occupation, or activity, of the Son in the life of the Trinity is glory. Let us see how this is so in the light of the above. The infinite perfection of the Father is His *objective* glory. The Son knows this perfection in Himself and in the Father; He knows that He has received it from the Father (*formal* glory). His *expressed* glory,

―――――
[4] Jn. 17:4.

telling the Father of His perfection, consists in His being the image of the Father (thus in His very Person of Son He is the glory of the Father) and His love of Him, since love is the greatest glory one can give. We have said that the function of a son is to please his father, but the glory that being the father's image and loving him perfectly give, is the best means to please him. Thus we can call the Son's function of pleasing the Father glory. If our life were only on the natural level, without the knowledge of the existence of the Trinity, God's knowledge and love of Himself would still be the image of our most necessary and important activities. But because we have been re-created in Christ by the divine life, the glory given to the Father by the Son is the pattern of what ours is to be.

We have seen how we rational creatures carry out our basic duty toward God. But what of the irrational creatures? We stated previously that in themselves they glorify God just by existing in accordance with His natural laws. They also glorify God through us, inasmuch as we, recognizing His perfection in nature, praise Him for it. For example, in the canticle of Lauds, the *Benedicite*, we are nature's "mouthpiece." "Worthy are you, O Lord our God, to reserve for yourself glory and honor and power; because you have created all things, and by your will they came into being and were created."[5] "The spirit of St. Francis in this particular finds dramatic expression in the first book of the *Fioretti* and in the loving view of the world with which Francis approached creatures, not with any eye of doubt or

---

[5] Apoc. 4:11.

misgiving but bestowing on them the title of brother and sister, as if they were born to find a place with him in the universal chant of praise and glory owed to the goodness of the Creator."[6] We shall consider more extensively the relation between man and material creation when we study the Mystical Body, mortification, and the gift of knowledge. At present it is only necessary to realize that we must use all creation to give God glory.

God's secondary end in creating man was man's own happiness, his good. But what is man's good? We spend our lives in the pursuit of good and we attain happiness insofar as the good we pursue is real or apparent. Our own frustrations should lead us back to this secondary motive of God in creating us. We must seek the real good if we are to be happy.

Philosophy teaches that every being seeks its own perfection, and St. Thomas shows that happiness lies in the perfection of man's highest faculties.[7] Man is composed of body and soul, and it is evident that the soul is his more important part, for it is not only the seat of his personality but it is also spiritual, indestructible. The soul has two faculties, intellect and will, which, because they pertain to the spiritual part of man, are his highest faculties. Therefore, happiness consists in the perfection of the intellect and the will.

How contrary is this notion of happiness to that of the world around us! How contrary, perhaps, to that

---

[6] Pacific Perantoni, O.F.M., *Franciscan Spirituality* (Chicago Franciscan Herald Press, 1950), p. 19.

[7] Cf. *Summa Theologica*, I, II, q. 3, a. 2.

which has actually motivated us in the past and which we shall constantly have to fight against! Happiness is so often regarded as the fulfillment of man's lower faculties, those of the body. Hence the existence in the world of such widespread frustration and unhappiness.

In order to perfect our highest faculties we must know their objectives. That of the intellect is truth — that which is. The intellect seeks to know all being; it is a boundless thirst for being, for everything that is. What it is really seeking is God, i.e., to know uncreated, infinite truth, infinite being. The more it knows God the more it is advancing toward happiness, because by its knowledge of God it is being perfected.

The object of the will is good. It is occupied in making choices. "What is the good here?" the will asks. "What is the greater good, the truly good?" The intellect knows truth and presents it to the will as good; the latter embraces it, unites itself to it. When the intellect presents God, infinite, perfect, being, to the will as the greatest good, and the will chooses this good above all others, uniting the whole person to the infinite good, the will is perfected and man's happiness is complete, for his highest faculties have been exercised upon infinite truth and good. Thus man is certain to be happy, for he is occupied with the eternal occupation of God, knowing and willing Himself. The life of God, His happiness, is the image of our happiness, for, since He created us according to the divine nature with an intellect and will, we can only be happy when both are exercised in the sole occupation of the divine intellect and will.

This is the philosophy of happiness, what it is in itself. But we do not exist in a hypothetical state of pure nature, but in a weakened nature that is the result of our first parents' defection from God. We are not more happy in this life because our weakened nature is too prone to seek its truth and good in self, rather than in God, and this in spite of God's gifts of revelation and grace. Our own experience proves the validity of the true nature of happiness: our happiest moments have been those when intellect and will rested in God.

The primary end of creation includes the acts of the secondary end. By the former we give God glory, which means that we know, pray to, love, and serve Him. By the latter we know Him and choose Him, and, since love is an operation of the will choosing another as good, we can conclude that our happiness consists in knowing and loving God. In knowing God in order to give Him glory we also know Him as our highest Good, and in giving Him the glory of love — the highest form of glory — we embrace Him as the object of our constant choice. We are happy in giving God glory.

Creation was motivated by God's glory, with regard to Himself, and by love, with regard to man. Our duty of glory is essentially that of love, which ceases to be a duty when our intellect realizes God's love for us, when it recognizes God as love.

INDIVIDUAL PRACTICES

1. Meditate on this basic fact: God is being from Him-

self, the creature is dependent for his being on God.

2. Meditate on the fact that God must act primarily only with reference to Himself.

3. Meditate on the fact that you exist only to give God glory.

4. Examine your habitual attitude toward God.

5. Examine your past attitude as to the purpose of your existence.

6. For one day realize how everything you do gives God glory.

7. Offer one Mass with the intention of giving God glory.

8. During the Office of one day realize that you are giving Him glory.

9. Examine yourself as to what really makes you happy, unhappy.

10. Meditate on the fact that your happiness and your duty of glory are identical.

GROUP QUESTIONS AND ACTIVITIES

1. What does St. Thomas mean by God's goodness?

2. How does suffering give God glory? How do mental sufferings caused by others' treatment of you, disappointments, the difficulties of the common life?

3. Why is love an act of choosing? With what human faculty do you essentially love?

4. Discuss real and apparent good.

5. Discuss: the cause of all unhappiness is choosing a good in opposition to God.

6. How can creatures help us give glory to God?

7. Psalms 110, 148, and 150 praise God for His creation. Find other psalms that do the same. Lauds is the hour

of praise. How do the psalms of Lauds fit this theme? Find psalms that express the idea that God is our happiness.

8. How does pertinent material in the Rule, Constitutions, and community Customaries relate to the themes of this chapter?

9. Discuss the idea of "praise of glory" in Sister Elizabeth of the Trinity.

CHAPTER 3

The Fulfillment of Glory

What I hope to achieve: *To realize that my duty of glory to God and my happiness will be perfectly fulfilled in the beatific vision, the goal of my life.*

To synthesize the previous chapters: *God created us as human beings in the image of His essence and as Christians in the likeness of His life. His primary purpose in creating us was that we should give Him glory: love, prayer, service. His secondary purpose was that we should be happy in giving Him this glory.*

The inner, triune life of God is our life. This is a postulate of the Christian life, a basic fact. We enter the life of the Trinity in the Son; therefore, our life is to be that of the Son in the Trinity. But this life is eternal glory to the Father, the glory of love and praise. This, then, is our end, and to it everything else must be directed and subordinated. This glory is eternal. We must keep this firmly in mind, because our tendency is to be primarily concerned with this time of trial, or, we may better say, this time of formation into likeness to the Son. Our difficulties result from our concentration on *this* life, with a vague and rather blurred idea of life after death. We must see always and as clearly as possible our end, which is glory, eternal, in, with, and through the Son. Then everything that happens to us now falls into place and has ultimate meaning. Then we can better understand what we ought to do now.

If God had willed that our lives be led on the purely natural level our knowledge of Him could be obtained only from reason. We would seek to know Him through our intellects and to choose Him with our wills, but we could discover God only in those perfections which are disclosed to us by creation. We could have no direct knowledge or experience of God, because this would be infinitely above our natural capabilities, as well as our desserts. Life after death would be that of Limbo: a place of natural happiness, with God known and loved, but only indirectly, as a conclusion to premises.

In elevating us as human beings to His own life, in raising the natural to the supernatural level, God willed to give us, as a foundation for our eternal occupation of glory, the beatific vision. "And this is the sum of eternal life — their knowing you, the only true God, and your ambassador Jesus Christ."[1]

The beatific vision is, strictly speaking, not a vision because we cannot "see" God. "See" implies the sense of sight. The beatific vision is knowing God in the same manner in which He knows Himself, that is, as

---
[1] Jn. 17:3.

He is. It is knowing Him clearly, directly, and intuitively, not through reason or revelation, but as He knows His divine Being. "We shall be like him, because we shall see him just as he is."[2] "We see now by means of a mirror in a vague way, but then we shall see face to face."[3] However, we cannot know Him in the same degree in which He knows Himself, i.e., comprehensively, for only God can do this.

Let us try to understand this a little better. Since the beatific vision is knowledge, we must consider what the act of knowing an object means. Human knowledge basically depends upon sense perceptions. From these an image is formed, and in the image the intellect discerns a meaning which it abstracts as an idea. For example, we see a single oak tree in a particular place in the yard. We form an image of this tree. This image is a type of knowledge, but is limited to a very particular tree. Specifically human knowledge requires the idea, which identifies this object in the imagination as being what it is, not a house nor a man, but a tree. For in forming the idea the intellect abstracts from the image the essential characteristics of the thing itself, what makes a tree a tree, in other words, its "treeness." Without the idea we would not know that this image represents a tree. We know by means of the idea.

In the beatific vision God does not give us an idea of Himself: He is Himself the idea whereby we know Him. That is, He unites His Essence, Himself, directly to our intellect, in the closest union possible to man.

---

[2] 1 Jn. 3:2.
[3] 1 Cor. 13:12.

This knowledge is intuitive, because it is not given through the senses and imagination, not even through the medium of faith. St. Thomas writes, ". . . if God's essense is to be seen at all, it must be that the intellect sees it through the divine essence itself; so that in that vision the divine essence is both the object and the medium of vision."[4]

This is the same manner in which God knows Himself. God is His own knowledge because He is indivisible.

Abbot Chapman writes: "If you ask in what it differs from Nirvana, I answer (with some hesitation) that it seems to be that the chief practical difference is that the Beatific Vision does not absorb the whole man into God, but leaves (nay intensifies) all his ordinary human faculties. It is an *addition* to his powers, not a substitution. The union is complete, but the human personality remains."[5]

Next we shall try to realize what is meant by knowing God *as He is in Himself*. A dog can know his master but never fully. He knows certain things about his master but not as he truly and completely *is*. Only another human being can do this to any extent, because a man knows another man *as a man knows*. Now in the beatific vision we creatures, infinitely lesser beings than God, are given the ability to know God as

---

[4] St. Thomas, *Summa Contra Gentiles*, III, ch. 51, in Anton Pegis, ed., *Basic Writings of Saint Thomas Aquinas* (New York: Random House, 1945), Vol. II, p. 92.

[5] Roger Hudleston, O.S.B., ed., *The Spiritual Letters of Dom John Chapman, O.S.B.* (New York: Sheed and Ward, 1946), p. 212.

He is, with the same knowledge by which He knows Himself. "Then I shall have complete knowledge, even as God has complete knowledge of me."[6]

The beatific vision is given to us as the foundation, the condition, of beatific love. Our wills, in the presence of infinite Good, choose It in a single, eternal act of love, giving our whole being to It, as It gives Itself to us. As God is the object and medium of our knowledge of God, so He is the medium of our love of God. The Holy Spirit, Love of Father and Son, will Himself be the love of us adopted sons. Then will be perfectly fulfilled the words of St. Paul, ". . . God's love is poured forth in our hearts by the Holy Spirit who has been given us."[7] The Trinitarian life will be complete in us. In the words of St. Ireneus, God will be ". . . seen, too, adoptively through the Son; and He shall also be seen paternally in the kingdom of heaven, the Spirit truly preparing man in the Son of God, and the Son leading him to the Father. . . ."[8]

Thus the primary purpose for which God created us, glory, will be ultimately attained. God will unite His being (objective glory) to our intellects directly. We shall know Him directly (formal glory) because of this union of His substance with our substance. And knowing Him as He is, our enraptured souls will embrace Him, eternally united to us, in eternal love, telling Him in a simple thought of the perfection of

---

[6] 1 Cor. 13:12.

[7] Rom. 5:5.

[8] St. Ireneus, *Adversus Haereses*, in A. Roberts and J. Donaldson, eds., *The Anti-Nicene Fathers* (New York: Charles Scribner's Sons, 1925), I, p. 489.

His being (expressed glory). For love and praise follow necessarily this knowledge.

But this is the very life of God — knowing and loving Him as He knows and loves Himself, i.e., by means of Himself. This is proper to God's own divine nature, for only He can do these two acts (which are in Him one act). "Therefore," St. Thomas writes in reference to the beatific vision, "this participation in a divine likeness is necessary in order that the divine substance be seen."[9] If we are to do what God alone does and can do, He must give us a share in His very nature. He has done this in baptism, the beginning of our eternal life of beatific glory. Sanctifying grace is in essence this glory.

"It is through this vision that we become most like God, and participators of His blessedness, since God understands His substance through His essence, and this is His blessedness."[10] St. Thomas is here referring to God's happiness, which shall be ours. Therefore in the life of beatific glory God's second purpose in creating us, our happiness, will be perfectly fulfilled: our intellects and wills will forever, permanently, possess their Object. The symbols, the mirror, in which we sought Him in faith, will give way to the Reality.

INDIVIDUAL PRACTICES

1. Is your life on the natural or supernatural level? Your motivation, God or self?
2. For one day see everything in it as related to beatific glory.

9 St. Thomas, op. cit., Pegis ed., Vol. II, p. 95.
10 Ibid., Vol. II, p. 93.

3. Meditate on your eternal occupation in heaven.
4. Meditate on the fact that your ultimate end is the glory you give God in the beatific vision, and that your happiness proceeds from this glory.
5. Form the habit of relating everything to the beatific vision.
6. Look to the future and see how living for beatific glory can give meaning to difficulties.
7. Meditate on the shortness of life.

GROUP QUESTIONS AND ACTIVITIES

1. Discuss: God deals with you only with reference to beatific glory.
2. What is the difference between such expressions as "getting to heaven," "saving your soul," and the beatific vision?
3. What is the relation between the duties, pleasures, and sufferings of our day and beatific glory?
4. How can beatific glory as your supernatural end influence your apostolic work after profession or ordination?
5. Did the human soul of Christ on earth enjoy the beatific vision?
6. Defend the fact that knowing God as He knows Himself makes you Godlike.

CHAPTER 4

God's Life in Us

What I hope to achieve: *To realize the nature of sanctifying grace, and thus to value it as the most important thing in my life.*

To synthesize the previous chapters: *God created us as human beings in the image of the divine essence, and as Christians in the likeness of His life. His primary purpose in creating us was that we should give Him the eternal glory of knowledge, love, and praise, as He knows, loves, and praises Himself. In this glory is our happiness.*

Beatific glory for us is participating in God's eternal act. For this, as we learned in the past chapter, we need, and are given by God's love, sanctifying grace. Also called habitual grace, it is a supernatural quality inherent in the soul, a state of soul, which makes us partakers of the divine nature and life.[1] It is a created share of God's life: "he has bestowed on us precious and very great promises, to enable us to . . . become partakers of the divine nature."[2]

[1] Cf. Adolphe Tanquerey, S.S., *The Spiritual Life* (Westminster: The Newman Press, 1930), no. 106.
[2] 2 Pet. 1:4.

Sanctifying grace is not, strictly speaking, God's life but a life similar to God's, otherwise we would be God. "We shall be like him, because we shall see him just as he is."[3] What God has given us is a created share in His life for the purpose of performing eternally the act of knowing and loving Him in His manner of knowing and loving Himself. "The soul is made like to God by grace."[4] The Greek Fathers Clement of Alexandria, St. Athanasius, and St. Basil call those in sanctifying grace "gods."

Sanctifying grace is not substantial to us, but accidental. St. Thomas explains this distinction with his usual clarity: "Now what is in God substantially comes to be accidentally in the soul participating in the divine goodness. . . ."[5] God's divine nature is necessary to Him or He would cease to be God. But it is not necessary to us as human beings. If it is given to us or taken away our essential human nature remains the same.

Sanctifying grace is, however, a *real* sharing in the divine nature in the sense that it elevates us above our nature so that we may know God as God knows Himself. There is nothing metaphorical here.

Sanctifying grace can only be explained in relation to the beatific vision; it is given to us only because of it. "We shall be like him, because we shall see him just as he is."[6] The beatific vision, then, is simply the flowering of sanctifying grace and the life of grace in

---

[3] 1 Jn. 3:2.

[4] *Summa Theologica*, I, q. 43, a. 5.

[5] *Ibid.*, I, II, q. 110, a. 2.

[6] 1 Jn. 3:2.

faith now is our heaven already begun. "Grace is nothing else than the beginning of glory in us."[7] "The life of grace, which has been given to us, is the seed of the life of heaven, and is the same life in its essence."[8]

But grace affects the whole man now. It is regarded as an "entitative habit," a new mode of being, similar to the human nature of Christ, totally affected by its union with the Person of the Son. As this union made Christ's human nature the most perfect human nature that ever existed, or will exist, and therefore most human, so sanctifying grace, elevating us to God's plane of life, in reality makes us the most complete of all human beings. All of our faculties, exercised for God, our Creator, eternal End, infinite Truth and Good, are perfectly fulfilled. As Mersch well puts it, ". . . since grace is a supreme consummation of being, we may say that grace is a supreme identification of a person with himself."[9]

We have been considering what theologians refer to as *created* grace, because it is a created share of the divine nature. There is another aspect of sanctifying grace, *uncreated* grace, which is the indwelling of the Holy Trinity in the soul, evident from the words of Christ, "Anyone who loves me will treasure my message, and my Father will love him, and we shall visit him and make our home with him."[10]

---

[7] *Summa Theologica*, II, II, q. 24, a. 3.

[8] R. Garrigou-Lagrange, O.P., *Christian Perfection and Contemplation* (St. Louis: B. Herder Book Co., 1939), p. 8.

[9] Émile Mersch, S.J., *The Theology of the Mystical Body* (St. Louis: B. Herder Book Co., 1951), p. 621.

[10] Jn. 14:23.

God is present in all creation, it is true, preserving and conducting each creature to its end. Since God is simple, His action cannot be separated from His being; hence He is omnipresent. But the Christian — and here we include all whom the Church considers as having at least baptism of desire — is the only creature whom God unites with His *nature*, i.e., the divine principle of knowing and loving God as He is. This union is founded not only on faith, but also on love or active faith. Hence the presence of God in the Christian in grace is the intimate presence of the One loved, on God's part a willing and enjoyed abiding. And as grace makes him an adopted son, the Father is present in him as his Father, the Son as his brother, the Holy Spirit as his spirit, i.e., the Holy Spirit is actively in him, forming the whole person by means of his supernaturalized intellect and will into the likeness of Christ. Here we see the Trinitarian "roles" in our regard as God's presence in the Christian in grace. In creation God is present to preserve and direct it to its end as creature; in the Christian He is present to enable him to perform his supernatural duty of Trinitarian glory, an activity which affects the whole person.

Msgr. Journet gives several figures which may clarify the relation of uncreated and created grace: "The indwelling of the divine Persons is, then, always the accompaniment of grace. The two mysteries are correlative. Grace is like a net we throw over the Trinity to hold it in captivity. Or here is another way to visualize it: when you bring into a room a source of light, it illuminates the walls; so, when the divine Persons come

34 A Synthesis of the Spiritual Life

to us (here we have the source, uncreated grace), they illuminate the walls of the soul (here we have the effect, created grace). And if you possess grace, then the source of grace, the three divine Persons, is there too. In the very gift of Sanctifying Grace, says St. Thomas, the Holy Spirit himself is sent and given to man to dwell in him. The uncreated Spirit is given in created grace, as the sun is given in its rays. The uncreated Gift of the Spirit and the created gift of grace are simultaneous. There are differences of degree in the life of individual souls; but in each of them the intensity of grace and the intensity of the indwelling increase with the same movement."[11]

The intimate presence of God in His people was a reward of the Covenant, now fully enjoyed in the new Covenant. In Leviticus we read: "If you live in accordance with my precepts, and are careful to observe my commandments . . . I will set my Dwelling among you, and will not disdain you. Ever present in your midst, I will be your God, and you will be my people."[12] This Word of God in Leviticus was later restated by the Word made flesh in John 14:23, quoted above.

The Holy Trinity is the source of sanctifying grace. St. Thomas says: "Now although, in God, to beget belongs to the Person of the Father, yet to produce any effect in creatures is common to the whole Trinity, by reason of the oneness of their nature: since, where there is one nature, there must needs be one power and

---

[11] Charles Journet, *The Meaning of Grace* (New York: P. J. Kenedy and Sons, 1960), p. 14.
[12] Lev. 26:3, 11–12.

one operation: whence our Lord says (John 5,19):
*What things soever the Father doth, these the Son also
doth in like manner.* Therefore it belongs to the whole
Trinity to adopt men as sons of God."[13]

"Like everything that is not God Himself, grace is
the work of the Three divine Persons, but that does
not hinder it from establishing us in personal relations
with each one of them . . . introducing us into their
own life."[14] This is possible because the Trinity is living
its life in us in uncreated grace, each Person acting
according to His Person in our regard. Created grace
has, as it were, taken us into the life of the Trinity,
and in uncreated grace the Father is our Father, the
Son is our brother in whom we are adopted sons, and
the Holy Spirit is our Spirit.[15]

Our end, beatific glory, is supernatural, and its beginning in us, sanctifying grace, elevates our nature to
the supernatural. By now we should realize that the
supernatural is in reality God's gift of Himself to us
that we might give ourselves to Him, in the Trinitarian
mode of giving.

13 *Summa Theologica*, III, q. 23, a. 2.
14 Jean Daujat, *The Theology of Grace* (New York: Haw-
thorne Books, 1959), p. 77.
15 We refer the novice masters and novice mistresses to F.
Prat, S.J., *The Theology of St. Paul* (Westminster: The Newman Bookshop, 1927), Vol. II, p. 291. Also to the articles by
P. De Letter, S.J., "Created Actuation by the Uncreated Act:
Difficulties and Answers," *Theological Studies*, Vol. 18, March,
1957, pp. 60–92; "Grace, Incorporation, Inhabitation," *Theological Studies*, Vol. 19, March, 1958, pp. 1–31; and to Charles
Davis, *Liturgy and Doctrine* (New York: Sheed and Ward,
1960), pp. 30–43. This last work is the most clear and comprehensive on this subject.

INDIVIDUAL PRACTICES

1. Meditate on the infinite gap that exists between God and you.
2. Meditate on the absolutely supernatural character of sanctifying grace; on the elevation of yourselves to a share in God's life.
3. Meditate on the effect of sanctifying grace on your whole day.
4. Make your recollection for a while the realization of God's presence within you and those with whom you come in contact.
5. Read Sister Elizabeth of the Trinity on the practice of the presence of God.
6. Meditate on the "roles" of the Trinity in your regard, God acting now in your soul.
7. Meditate on the relation between uncreated and created grace.

GROUP QUESTIONS AND ACTIVITIES

1. Discuss the various concepts Catholics have of sanctifying grace.
2. How can the true nature of sanctifying grace be taught? Let one person give a demonstration lesson or sermon.
3. Discuss sanctifying grace as an "entitative habit," affecting the whole life of the whole person.
4. Discuss the fact that sanctifying grace is the most important thing in your lives.
5. Find references to God's presence in the psalms.
6. Discuss the distinction between uncreated and created grace.
7. Discuss the supernatural as God's gift of Himself to you.

CHAPTER 5

Through Christ

What I hope to achieve: To realize that through the priestly sacrifice of Christ we receive beatific glory, sanctifying grace, the beginning of that glory, and all the supernatural means to it.

To synthesize the previous chapters: Our end and our happiness is to give God glory as He does Himself. This requires a share in God's life.

"But when the designated period of time had elapsed, God sent his Son, born of a woman, born in subjection to the Law, in order to redeem those who were in subjection to the Law, that we might receive the adoption."[1] Although written with a very particular end in view, this passage of St. Paul contains the elements of the redemption: the Father sent the Son, made man, to be the mediator of man's atonement for sin and of God's restoration to him of the beatific vision.

Adam, head of the human race, had sinned, and his sin persisted in its effects in his descendants. Added to the original sin were the innumerable personal sins,

---

[1] Gal. 4:4.

the rejections of God, of fallen man. The most serious personal effect of Adam's sin was his loss for himself and his posterity of the original end intended for them by God, the beatific vision. Justice demanded that man atone to God for his sins. But justice did not demand that God restore the beatific vision to him. This was a supernatural gift, God's special gift of Himself to the human race. No matter what atonement man made, if the beatific vision were to be given back to him, it would only be because of God's love.

"So marked, indeed, has been God's love for the world that he gave his only-begotten Son. . . ."[2] It was God's intention to restore to man his supernatural end through his atonement in the Person of the Son made man. The Son was, therefore, to be mediator.

Mediator means one who holds a middle position between others. Jesus Christ is the one mediator between God and us, for He is God as well as man like us. "For there is but one God and one Mediator between God and men, Christ Jesus, himself man, who gave himself a ransom for all. . . ."[3]

Man alone could never have made adequate atonement for his sins. The formal rejection of God, which is sin, is an offense of the creature against the Creator; it is the finite turning from the Infinite and choosing the finite. Even in a small matter, venial sin, isn't this rejection something for which man can never *justly* make satisfaction? Adam's turning from God remained in the race as the primary sin demanding atonement.

---

[2] Jn. 3:16.
[3] 1 Tim. 2:5.

But the race was powerless, because it was a creature and, as finite, incapable of making true atonement.

God chose a people, who were to be His, as He was theirs, and by His word they looked forward to an ideal kingdom, to be ruled by One who would be anointed King, Son, and Mediator of the atonement. Isaia described this Messia-King as the suffering Servant of Yahweh.

"But he was pierced for our offenses, crushed for our sins; upon him was the chastisement that makes us whole, by his stripes we were healed."[4] The atonement would not be for the elect people only. Israel was to be a missionary people, giving the Good News, for "In you shall all the nations of the earth be blessed."[5] The promise to Abraham would be fulfilled in the mystery of Christ.[6]

The Mediator had to be God and man, for equal satisfaction had to be made: it must come from man, for he had sinned, and it must be of infinite value, for God had been offended. Only an infinite atonement would be adequate.

Why was the Son the mediator? St. Thomas gives as one reason the fact that the redeemed are to be sons. "Hence it was fitting that by Him who is the natural Son, men should share this likeness of sonship by adoption."[7] He is the Mediator because He is the Son. "Simi-

---

[4] Isa. 53:5.

[5] Gen. 12:3.

[6] Cf. Albert Gélin, P.S.S., *The Religion of Israel* (New York: Hawthorn Books, 1958), Chap. 5.

[7] *Summa Theologiae*, III, q. 3, art. 8.

larly Christ did not seek for himself the glory of becoming the high priest, but God said to him: 'You are my Son; today have I become your Father.'"[8] The Son made man pleases the Father by the glory of His human obedience, which is His filial love in action. "To do the will of him whose ambassador I am, and to complete the work he has assigned — that is my food!"[9] Later Christ will send the Holy Spirit, but for the initial mission, that of Mediator, the sacrificial obedience of the incarnate Son is required.

The union of divine nature with human nature necessary for the role of Mediator is called the hypostatic union. This means, as we know, that there are in Christ one Person and two complete natures. He has, in addition to His divine nature, a perfect human nature consisting of a soul and a body. Consequently He has a divine intellect and a human intellect, a divine will and a human will. But, and on this we do not sufficiently meditate and pray, His human nature does not have its own "person." It has been from the instant of the Incarnation assumed, taken into, the Person of the Son. If we understand by nature the *principle* of action, person is the *agent* of action. I have human nature, the equipment to act as a human being; when I act by means of this nature, I am acting as a person, me. Christ's human nature, even though He has soul and body, is not its own agent of action. If it were, everything He did as man would be done by a man only, would have only finite value. Hence, His atonement

8 Hebr. 5:5.
9 Jn. 4:34.

would not have been adequate, and we would not have been redeemed. The agent of His action as man had to be His Person of Son if He was to be the Mediator. We shall return to this point again, but at present we would like to point out that besides being necessary for redemption, the hypostatic union was also fitting, because of the nature of sin. Man, from Adam on, turned from God by his will, choosing for his good an object other than God; Christ, in His sacrificial obedience, united His human will with the divine, choosing God.

Christ's atonement for His brothers was accomplished through His priestly sacrifice. The cross was the altar, Christ both priest and victim; on it He offered Himself as the only acceptable victim, to be immolated as a sacrificial victim must be, man's atonement to God. The redemption, therefore, was achieved essentially by the passion and death of Christ. The whole of His earthly life prior to the crucifixion was one oblation of Himself to the Father for His death, and because of this sacrificial oblation every act or "mystery" was a source of grace. But the sacrifice consisted in His death. The efficacious value of the Resurrection we shall consider in the next chapter.

The priestly sacrifice of Christ was accomplished once, but it is still present in the Church. The Mass is the active presence of His offering and sacrifice of Himself and of its infinite effects. It is a memorial, but a dynamic memorial, for at the Consecration Christ becomes both priest and victim, offering His life and death to the Father. True, we receive thereby "every heavenly blessing and grace," but as we members unite with our Head in offering Himself, He offers us, His members, as co-victims, whose sacrifice acquires value only in His. Mass, to us, must be first of all this redemptive sacrifice, for only this is its essence.

Christ, God-Man, is the Mediator of our atonement. His satisfaction for sin more than equaled the offense: it was infinite in its effects and in its merits. He is, therefore, the Mediator of our justification, sanctifying grace, the state of holiness because it is God's life, and of the full development of that life, beatific glory. He is the Mediator of means to active holiness, and therefore to the increase of the divine life: the supernatural virtues, the gifts, and actual grace.

How do we receive sanctifying grace and the other supernatural means? Grace, the virtues, and the gifts are given to us initially in baptism. This is the purpose not only of baptism, but also of the other sacraments: to give us the created sharing in God's life and the means to its development. If lost they are given again by Penance and Extreme Unction, and increased by the other sacraments. No matter what the particular sacramental grace is or the other effects, the chief purpose of the sacraments is to contain and give sanctifying grace. They have been defined as acts of Christ. We can say that they are the redemptive act of Christ, for His redemption operates through their outward signs. "So from His own side Christ built up His Church, just as Eve was produced from the side of Adam. . . . For, as God made woman to be produced from the side, so Christ gave to us from His own side the water and blood by which the Church was renewed."[10]

We must note here that grace, the virtues, and the gifts are also increased by every good act done for a supernatural motive: love of God, hope in God, fear of God. Since hope presupposes love of God, and our fear of Him is reverential, that of a son, love must be joined to the latter two motives in order to merit this increase. A virtual intention (e.g., the good intention of the morning offering, made once, but not renewed before each action, whose influence is still active) suffices, although, practically, the actual intention, at least before each important or different activity, should be made, as a reminder that we are doing this for God.

Christ is also the Mediator of our adoration, the adorer *par excellence.* As man He has a created soul and body; therefore, as man He adores the Father with an adoration that has an infinite value because it proceeds from a divine Person. Not until the Incarnation did the Father possess a perfect adorer. Now Christ as priest for the human race mediates, offers, our feeble adoration, which passing to the Father *through Him* is pleasing and acceptable because united to His own.

Lastly, Christ is Mediator of our whole duty of glory. With His perfect human intellect enlightened by His knowledge of the Father which He has by reason of the beatific vision, He alone can give the Father perfect glory. He alone can *tell* the Father what He is, alone can love with full knowledge of infinite Good, with the

---

[10] St. John Chrysostom, *Homily to the Neophytes,* in *The Lessons of the Temporal Cycle and the Principal Feasts* (St. Meinrad: Abbey Press, 1941), p. 393.

utter giving of self that is perfect love. And as with our adoration, so in transmitting our glory He infinitely increases its value.

"But when the designated period of time had elapsed, God sent His Son, born of a woman . . ." and that woman was Mary. She furnished God the Son with a body for the sacrifice. The Precious Blood was from her. Hence Leo XIII called Mary "the co-operator in the sorrowful expiation made for the human race."[11] From her knowledge of Scripture Mary knew that the Messia would be the Redeemer, hence her *"Fiat"* was also consent to share as much as she was able in the redemption.

On Calvary she united her intellect and will with the intentions of Christ, her sufferings to His. All of her sufferings in His regard were in view of His role of Redeemer. "Free from all sin, original and personal, always most intimately united with her Son, as another Eve she offered Him on Golgotha to the Eternal Father for all the children of Adam sin-stained by his fall, and her mother's rights and mother's love were included in the holocaust."[12]

Of themselves the sufferings and love of Mary were of no value. But united to the Redemption of her Son they serve as the merits of the human being of greatest worth and dignity, of the first expiator among men. And since she has no need of expiation, her merits are for her children. She offers more than her love and sufferings: she offers her Son.

---

[11] *Acta Apostolica Sedis*, XXVII, p. 176.

[12] Pius XII, *Mystici Corporis* (Washington: National Catholic Welfare Conference, 1943), no. 107.

The Trinity is the source of our divine life, Christ is the meritorious cause, for it comes to us by His Blood from the cross. All that we have supernaturally is *through* Christ. With reason our prayers addressed to the Father end "through Christ our Lord." Through Him we receive the ability to give God glory in the beatific vision, and through Him, the Mediator, comes our own glory. "Through Him, with Him, in Him, is to Thee, God the Father, in the unity of the Holy Spirit, all honor and glory!"

INDIVIDUAL PRACTICES

1. Meditate on the nature of sin.
2. Meditate on Isaia 53.
3. Meditate on the fittingness of the Son as Mediator.
4. Notice the crucifixes in the house, remembering each time that they represent Christ as Mediator.
5. Offer the Mass, aware that it is Christ offering to the Father His sacrificial death.
6. Perform, with permission, some penance, uniting it to the infinite atonement of Christ.
7. Say the Joyful Mysteries, meditating in each on Christ's offering of Himself to the Father.
8. Meditate on the *Stabat Mater*.

GROUP QUESTIONS AND ACTIVITIES

1. Why should mortal sin result in the loss of sanctifying grace?
2. Study the term "Son of Man" in Daniel 7, and Christ's use of it for Himself.

3. Study the Messianic psalms.
4. Discuss the idea and elements of sacrifice in the Old Testament.
5. Study the Mass, relating its four ends to Christ's redemptive sacrifice.
6. Write as a composite effort, a Stations of the Cross with Christ as priest and victim of the sacrifice as theme.
7. Discuss your duty of reparation to God. Why is it necessary? Why should it be a joy for you?
8. Discuss the right of the Blessed Mother to the title of co-redeemer.

CHAPTER 6

In Christ

> **What I hope to achieve:** *To realize that I form with Christ and the other members of the Mystical Body one person.*
> **To synthesize the previous chapters:** *Our end and our happiness is to give God glory as He does Himself. This requires a share in His life, which has been merited for us by the sacrifice of Christ.*

We cannot consider the redemption only as meriting; if Christ's sacrifice is to have meaning and purpose, redemption must also mean giving the effects of that sacrifice. Christ merited by His life prior to His death and essentially by that death; He gave and gives by His risen life. That is the meaning of these texts of St. Paul: "The last Adam became a spirit imparting life." "This Good News concerns his Son, who as regards the flesh was born of the line of David, but according to the spirit of holiness was constituted the mighty Son of God by his resurrection from the dead, Jesus Christ our Lord."[1]

Before the resurrection, Christ's body felt the de-

---

[1] 1 Cor. 15:45; Rom. 1:3–4.

mands of the body, was bound by its needs, suffered
from its weaknesses. It was in this condition that He
merited. Although, because of the hypostatic union, His
body was always that of God, and therefore God, for
the purpose of the redemption it had to share the human burden. The resurrection made it what the body
of God should be: totally taken over by the divine
nature, freed from human necessities, completely given
to God. ". . . the life that he lives is a life for God."[2]
And as His body was a source of merit before, it now
becomes a source of life, of that same life for God.[3]

"Christ, therefore, is 'constituted Son of God' by His
resurrection. This statement does not imply that now
for the first time Christ becomes 'Son of God' in the
depths of His being. He was always God's Son in that
sense (cf. Rom. 1:3). The meaning is rather that Christ's
sonship is now seen in relation to us; through resurrection He becomes capable of sharing His sonship
with us."[4]

At the resurrection Christ's human nature for the
first time experienced the full influence of the divine
nature that is in the Person of the Son. No longer
need it feel the demand for sleep and food, no more
would it suffer. The humiliation of experimental knowledge is past. Now it is glorified because it has become

---

[2] Rom. 6:10.

[3] Cf. F. X. Durrwell, C.SS.R., The Resurrection (New York:
Sheed and Ward, 1960), p. 99. Also Summa Theologica, III,
q. 56, a. 2.

[4] Stanislaus Lyonnet, S.J., "Redemption through Death and
Resurrection," Worship, April, 1961, p. 282. The whole article
should be read.

what the human nature of the Son should be. The divine being of the Son impregnates every cell. Hence. we can say that because of this, the human nature of Christ did not experience the fullness of the Sonship of its Person until the resurrection, and, therefore, Christ could not give to the human race the created share of the divine nature until He, the First-Born, had received the full effects of His own divine nature in the humanity that He has in common with man.

The redemptive act is, then, twofold. Christ "was delivered up for our sins, and rose again for our sanctification."[5] His death and resurrection were both instrumental causes of our redemption: the former was the means of meriting; the latter, the means of giving the redemption to those who are united with His risen self.

Therefore, because Christ is for us the instrumental source of the divine life, He holds a position in relation to us analogous to that between our head and the rest of our body: both Christ and our head have in common the fact that they are sources of life.

The metaphor *Mystical Body* expresses the reality and nature of our relation to Christ. It is defined as the Church organically united to Christ, as the body is to the head. Our union with Him is more than a moral one, such as exists between club members. It is a necessary union, organic, because we are dependent on Him, just as the parts of our body are dependent on our head, for life. The principle of the Mystical Body is sanctifying grace.

Christ expresses this vital relationship in the terms

[5] Rom. 4:25.

of vine and branches: "I am the real vine, and my Father is the vinedresser. He prunes away any branch of mine that bears no fruit, and cleans any branch that does bear fruit, that it may bear yet more abundant fruit. By now you are clean, thanks to the lessons I have given you. Remain united with me, and I will remain united with you. A branch can bear no fruit of itself, that is, when it is not united with the vine; no more can you, if you do not remain united with me. I am the vine, you are the branches. One bears abundant fruit only when he and I are mutually united; severed from me, you can do nothing."[6]

St. Paul is the first to express the relationship between Christ and His followers as that between *head* and *members*. "He [the Father] has subjected every single thing to his authority and has appointed him sovereign head of the Church, which is truly his body, the complement of him who fills all the members with all graces."[7] "For example, just as the body is a unit, although it has many members, and all the members of the body, many though they are, form but one body, so too is the Christ."[8] ". . . because the husband is head of the wife just as Christ is head of the Church and also savior of that body."[9] "Further, he is the head of his body, the Church, in that he is the beginning, the first to rise from the dead, so that he may have pre-eminence over every creature. For it pleased God the Father that in him all fullness should dwell, and

---

[6] Jn. 15:1–5.
[7] Eph. 1:22–23.
[8] 1 Cor. 12:12.
[9] Eph. 5:23.

that through him God should reconcile to himself every being, and make peace both on earth and in heaven through the blood shed on the cross."[10]

St. Augustine, who could be called the Doctor of the Mystical Body, was bold but precise when he called that body the "whole Christ." "All mankind is in Christ one man, and the unity of Christians is one Man." "Our Lord Jesus Christ is as one whole perfect man, both head and body."[11] The expressions are bold, but point out the logical conclusion that between Christ and His Church there is not only a union of dependence, but also a union, a oneness, of life. Head and members live by the same life; they live the same life.

The term *head* conveys, besides the idea of life, that of direction, for the head contains in itself all the senses, whereas the rest of the body has only the sense of touch. Christ, in addition to being the source of the divine life, is guide to the Mystical Body.

At the moment of the Incarnation Christ's human nature was united to the divine in such a manner that it could not have its own "personality," or quality of being a person. The person of Christ was the Person of the Son. The hypostatic union conferred divinity on His human nature, taking it into the life of God. Flowing into His human soul, because of this union, and simultaneous with it was His own created grace. In the Mystical Body there exists a oneness of life, not the same divine life that is in Christ as a divine Person,

---

[10] Col. 1:18–20.
[11] In Erich Przywara, S.J., *An Augustine Synthesis* (New York: Harper and Brothers, Publishers, 1958), pp. 217, 218.

nor the same sanctifying grace as His own, but a oneness nonetheless because the divine life which He gives
us is *of the same kind* as His created grace. It is
impossible to make us God, but possible to make us
Godlike, able to know and love Him as He knows and
loves Himself. There is oneness of life of head and
members because of the oneness of our eternal activity.
There is in us, too, oneness of life with the whole
Trinity, uncreated grace.

"But if anyone is taken up and incorporated into
Christ's sacred humanity, he is given a part in the
new way, the supernaturally perfect way of being man.
He receives a sort of new nature, a super-nature which
is the divinization of simple nature, and shares in the
way of being man that is proper to Christ and that is
His with so great an abundance that He can enrich
every man with it."[12] We receive in the Mystical Body
a oneness with Christ's human nature, which is an
elevation, a divinization, of our own, because something happens to us that is similar to what hap-
pened to the human nature when it was united to
the divine.

Third, in the Mystical Body there is a union of likeness: we are given the ability to be like our head,
physically and morally. Physical (but not material) likeness means that the same supernatural endowments are
given to us that were given to Christ's human nature:
sanctifying grace, that is, the divine life, the seven infused virtues, and the seven gifts. The virtues and gifts

---

[12] Émile Mersch, S.J., *The Theology of the Mystical Body* (St.
Louis: B. Herder Book Co., 1951), p. 611.

are in Christ, abiding in Him in their fullness because He is their source, and are infused in us who are one with Him. The divine life in its created form is there for us as a new species of life. We have what Christ has; our principle of life is the same as His. "In the faithful soul," writes Bishop Myers, "this sanctifying grace, with its retinue of virtues and gifts, may, of course, be increased by meritorious good works, and thus the likeness to Christ increases."[13] Moral likeness we shall consider in the next chapter.

Therefore, because of our union with Christ in His Mystical Body, because we form with Him the "whole Christ," we become by adoption what He is by nature — sons. "Out of love he predestined us for himself to become through Jesus Christ his adopted children, conformably to the good pleasure of his will, to the praise of his resplendent grace, with which he has adorned us in his beloved Son."[14]

The Father willed that we come to the Trinity in the Mystical Body. But this body is the complete body of the Person of His Son. Therefore, our relations with Him as Christians are only possible through the Son, in Him, and with Him. His relations with us are only those of the Father to His Son. We may say, then, that the Father knows and loves us as Christians only in relation to the Son. Now we see the Mystical Body in its essential meaning: to be to the Father His Son.

The Trinitarian image of our life was expressed by

---

[13] Bishop E. Meyers, "The Mystical Body of Christ," in *The Teaching of the Catholic Church* (New York: The Macmillan Company, 1958), Vol. II, p. 670.

[14] Eph. 1:5–6.

Christ in His prayer after the Last Supper: "All are
to be one; just as you, Father, are in me and I am in
you, so they, too, are to be one in us. . . . The world
must come to acknowledge that I am your ambassador,
and that you love them as you love me."[15] We are to
the Father His Son, because of our oneness with Him.
He loves us as His Son, and this love is, therefore,
the personified love of Father and Son, the Holy
Spirit. ". . . God's love is poured forth in our hearts
by the Holy Spirit who has been given us."[16]

The Holy Spirit is not only the Father's gift to us,
but also the Son's. He is given to us by the Father,
through and in the Son. "Christ, as man, possessed the
fullness of the Spirit and was to cause it to be poured
out upon us as soon as he had accomplished his redemptive work. Then, at the moment of the resurrection, he becomes actually for himself and for us a
'quickening spirit'; for himself, since the grace with
which he abounds fills his body and renders it spiritual,
and for us, because he communicates to us lavishly al
the gifts of the Holy Spirit and the Holy Spirit Himself. Henceforth, from the supernatural point of view,
we live by the Son and also by the Spirit; or, more
exactly, we live by the Spirit sent by the Son."[17]

The role of the Holy Spirit in our regard is His
Trinitarian role of love. Father and Son, loving each
other in the Holy Spirit, give themselves to each other.
He is their dynamic love, and so He is for us. That

[15] Jn. 17:21, 23.   [16] Rom. 5:5.
[17] F. Prat, S.J., The Theology of St. Paul (Westminster, Md.:
The Newman Bookshop, 1927), Vol. II, p. 293.

we might give ourselves to the Son and, in Him, to the Father, the Spirit incorporates us in Christ, giving us the divine life. St. Athanasius wrote that ". . . by the communication of the Spirit we become sharers of the divine nature . . ." and St. Gregory Thaumaturgus rhapsodized concerning Him, "Image of the Son . . . life, cause of the living; holy fountain; holiness, dispenser of holiness; in whom God the Father is manifested. . . ."[18] Thus, by the Spirit, we are able to give ourselves to the Father in the Person of His Son. "Whoever are led by the Spirit of God, they are the sons of God."[19] ". . . God adopts us as sons by giving us his Spirit, and Christ adopts us as brother by sending us his Spirit. . . . The proof that 'you are sons, is that God hath sent the Spirit of his Son into your hearts, where he cries: Abba, Father!' "[20]

The Holy Spirit is, therefore, the soul of the Mystical Body, for as the human soul is the principle within us which vivifies the whole person, so He as the giver of the divine life, the virtues and the gifts, is the one who gives supernatural life to the Mystical Body, its very *raison d'être*. From Pentecost until the second coming, the risen Christ and the Holy Spirit are active: the former as the head, the latter as the soul of the "whole Christ."

The basic concept of the Church is that of the Mystical Body. ". . . he is the head of his body, the Church."[21] "If we would define and describe this true Church of Jesus Christ — which is the One, Holy,

[18] *Patrologia Graeca*, 26, col. 585; 10, col. 984.
[19] Rom. 8:14.   [20] Prat, *loc. cit.*   [21] Col. 1:18.

Catholic, Apostolic, Roman Church — we shall find no
expression more noble, more sublime or more divine
than the phrase which calls it 'the Mystical Body of
Jesus Christ.' "[22] This is the definition of Pius XII in
his encyclical *Mystici Corporis.*

All Catholics are in the Mystical Body, but what of
non-Catholics? Christ is the head of all men except
the damned. Therefore He is head of the saints, of
the souls in purgatory, of His members on earth, and
potentially of all the others. Someone who is not now a
member may be one before his death and, hence, will
be eternally a part of the "whole Christ." Catholics
who are in mortal sin are atrophied members. In practice, therefore, we should see all persons as Christ.

Lastly, we must realize the relation between Christ
as head and nonrational creation. St. Paul wrote to
the Ephesians: "And this good pleasure he decreed to
put into effect in Christ when the designated period
of time had elapsed, namely to gather all creation both
in heaven and on earth under one head, Christ."[23]
How are all things to be reheaded in Christ? By our
Christian use of them. Every creature which helps us
give God glory, and essentially the glory of love, is taken
up into the Mystical Body and is under the headship
of Christ. From the constellations to the food we eat,
creation is a means of prayer, love, and service.
"Whether, then, you eat or drink, or do anything else,
do everything for God's glory."[24]

The Mystical Body was eternally in the divine mind,

[22] *Mystici Corporis*, no. 13.
[23] Eph. 1:10.　　　　　　　　　[24] 1 Cor. 10:31.

the union of creation with the Father in Christ —
Christ, the link, the head, the center. "Further, he is
the head of his body, the Church, in that he is the
beginning, the first to rise from the dead, so that he may
have pre-eminence over every creature. For it pleased
God the Father that in him all fullness should dwell,
and that through him God should reconcile to himself
every being, and make peace both on earth and in
heaven through the blood shed on the cross."[25] Upon
this doctrine of the Mystical Body our spiritual life
must be founded.

INDIVIDUAL PRACTICES

1. Meditate on the risen Christ as source of the divine
   life.

2. Meditate on the mystery of the "whole Christ."

3. What influence has it had on your life?

4. For one day make your recollection a realization that
   you are living by life received from Christ the head.

5. For one day make a special effort to see everyone as
   Christ.

6. Offer your human nature to Christ, as He offered His
   to His divine nature.

7. Meditate on the fact that because of the Mystical
   Body one "shares in the way of being man that is
   proper to Christ."

8. Meditate on your physical likeness to Christ.

9. Meditate on the role of the Holy Spirit in the Mystical Body.

---

[25] Col. 1:18–20.

GROUP QUESTIONS AND ACTIVITIES

1. Discuss the redemptive value of the resurrection.

2. Discuss the fact that Christ's human nature has no "personality" of its own, but belongs totally to the Person of the Son.

3. What are the similarities between your incorporation into Christ and the hypostatic union? (As the human nature is directed by the Person of the Son, so we members of the Mystical Body must be directed by Christ our Head. Cf. Bérulle in Brémond's *Literary History of Religious Thought in France*, III, p. 69 ff.)

4. Relate the visible Church to the Mystical Body; the community; this house.

5. Discuss: what is written of Christ's human nature in Scripture and the liturgy is also, in a way, written of you. Cf. the prayer *Deus, qui humanae substantiae* of the Offertory, for example.

6. Discuss: "Upon this doctrine of the Mystical Body our spiritual life must be founded."

7. Why was this doctrine not stressed in the past three centuries?

8. Let each prepare a short talk on the Mystical Body, each directed to a different audience.

9. Discuss the fact that the Mystical Body is the fulfillment of the "people of God" of the Old Testament.

CHAPTER 7

With Christ

What I hope to achieve: *To realize that I must be another Christ for the Father.*
To synthesize the previous chapters: *My duty of glory and my happiness will be effected in the beatific vision and in my life now in Christ as a member of His Mystical Body, because it is through Him I have received the divine life.*

We must be for the Father His Son. That is the theme of this book, that is the synthesis of our spiritual life, unifying all its elements. We must be for the Father, insofar as the Holy Spirit gives us the ability, another Christ. The Father, whose eternal occupation is knowing and loving His being in the Son, seeks to know and love this being in us. The Son is the image of the Father: "He who sees me sees the Father."[1] He is the image of God in whom we have been re-created. Therefore, our occupation now is to reproduce in ourselves the divine being that is in Christ.

"Be perfect, then, as your heavenly Father is perfect."[2]

---

[1] Jn. 14:9.
[2] Mt. 5:48.

59

Christ, the image of the Father, the Word expressing the Father's infinite being, by possessing a human soul and body, has given us a concrete image of perfection. "He is the image of the invisible God. . . ."[3] In imitating Christ we are pleasing to the Father not only because we are conforming ourselves to His perfection, but also because we are doing so according to the exemplar He has given us.

His human nature gives us actions, states, and words to imitate and live by. In particular, He has given us the interior life of His human soul, including His virtues, to make our own. His human life is a perfect image of the Father's perfection.

Therefore, in every way Christ's life is ours: it is our exemplar and our source, ours to follow and to live by. In the Mystical Body we do what the Son does, because our means — grace, the virtues, and the gifts, which are in Him in their fullness — are similar to His own. Bishop Myers has clarified this point: "For being informed, being vitalized by the same supernatural life, we are disposed to the same supernatural activity as Christ himself: that is to say, the infused supernatural habits (the seven virtues) dispose the soul to the same operations, freely performed, as those elicited by Christ: the Christian by acting in accordance with those virtues, imitates or follows Christ. We are thus united to Christ in thought and word and deed, striving to look at all things as Christ Himself would have looked at them, to speak of all as Christ would have spoken, to behave to all as Christ would have behaved

---
[3] Col. 1:15.

— thus becoming 'other Christs.' Christ became the living standard of holiness, the divine example which we strive to reproduce in ourselves."[4]

We have, therefore, within us the same supernatural means that are in the human nature of Christ — divine life, virtues, gifts. If we live this life by means of the virtues, guided by the Holy Spirit's gifts, we will inevitably be able to say, "It is now no longer I who live, but Christ lives in me."[5] Commenting on this passage, the sixteenth-century theologian Cardinal Cajetan wrote: "For he who is crucified with Christ has Christ as the reason for all his actions; Christ so directs, disposes, and uses his internal and external faculties that he can justly say: 'Christ lives in me.'"[6]

"My dear children, I am again suffering the pangs of childbirth for you, until Christ is formed within you!"[7] St. Cyril of Alexandria wrote of this verse: "He is formed by means of the Spirit, Who regenerates us for God through Himself."[8] The Holy Spirit unites us to Christ our head, who gives us the divine life through the Spirit. From the beginning, from our baptism, Christ is formed in us, or, rather, we are formed in Christ, for we are at once adopted as sons, we are elevated to His life, we are, as it were, taken into the Trinity in His Person. By being incorporated in Him, we have put on Christ. All of this is a free gift on

---

[4] "The Mystical Body of Christ," in *Teaching of the Catholic Church* (New York: The Macmillan Company, 1958), Vol. II, pp. 670–671.

[5] Gal. 2:20.

[6] In Émile Mersch, S.J., *The Whole Christ* (Milwaukee: The Bruce Publishing Co., 1938), p. 515.

[7] Gal. 4:19. [8] *Patrologia Graeca*, 75, col. 1089.

God's part. We have been given this new state, this new mode of being. But we cannot say, "I am in the Mystical Body, therefore, I am another Christ for the Father," and go on living our own life with no reference to Christ's. We must *live* our new mode of being, our state of being another Christ. In other words, the formation of Christ in us is a life process. The Holy Spirit is continually forming us into Christ, but with our co-operation. The divine life has re-created us in Christ's image, but the day-to-day operation of the infused virtues and the gifts forms us gradually into His likeness.

This likeness to the image of Christ is the result of love: of the love of the Father for us and of our love, prompted by and joined to "the love of the Spirit."[9] Hence, the role of the Holy Spirit in the Trinity — love — is, in our regard, to make us essentially by love into Christ. Christ's Spirit is within us, dynamic and untiring love, unceasing until we become with all our will a son to the Father.

There is an imitation of Christ that we shall call "exterior" imitation. This is the same as the imitation of a purely human model who appeals to us, e.g., our patron saint. In taking the latter for a moral exemplar we would study our patron to such an extent that we would attempt to become a reproduction. In the "exterior" imitation of Christ we pattern ourselves after His example and words: we study Him and try to become another Christ. Although grace is always most necessary in this imitation, we still conceive of it as

[9] Rom. 15:30.

an exterior process: we look at our model and we imitate.

However, because of sanctifying grace and the Mystical Body, our imitation of Christ must be differently orientated. It is primarily an interior process, Christ living in and through us. The result of "exterior" imitation would probably be the same. But what a difference in viewpoint! I am not outside of Christ, imitating Him; I am *in* Him because I am in the whole Christ, and I am only reproducing the life that my head has lived and wants to live *now*. Christ's life, therefore, is not a life which was lived once and is now merely to be imitated, but a life that continues to be lived by His members.

St. John Eudes wrote: "It necessarily follows (from the doctrine of the Mystical Body) that, just as the members are animated by the spirit of the head, and live the same life, so you must also be animated by the spirit of Jesus, live His life, walk in His ways, be clothed with His sentiments and inclinations, and perform all your actions in the dispositions and intentions that actuated His. In a word, you must carry on and perpetuate the life, religion and devotion which He exercised upon earth."[10]

We must "live His life," or, rather, co-operate with Him living it in us and through us. Why is this? First, because He is our exemplar. His whole life is for us the pattern of our holiness, our likeness to it the norm of our acceptance by the Father. If we allow

[10] St. John Eudes, *The Kingdom of Jesus* (New York: P. J. Kenedy and Sons, 1946), p. 3.

our head to relive His mysteries, His words, and, above all, His interior life, we are certain to be pleasing to the Father. Second, because our love for Him prompts us to unite ourselves to every precious detail of His earthly life, to beg Him to relive it in and through us as the most effective way of imitation. Third, because He wills us to relive this life in order to give us the graces merited by each mystery. (We shall consider this point further on in this chapter.) Fourth, because we have been given the very vital principle of Christ's life, the Holy Spirit, who gives us sanctifying grace, the virtues, the gifts, and actual grace.

Every man's life consists of two elements, the exterior and the interior: his bodily actions, sufferings and words; and his thoughts, desires, fears, intentions, and virtues. So it is with Christ's life, and as the interior is the more important element of the two, springing as it does from the intellect and will, Christ's interior life is more worthy of our attention, for it gave meaning and value to His exterior acts. In considering His interior we must begin with His intentions. Actually there was only one — glory to the Father —but for practical purposes we can assign to Him two: glory and redemption. From our study of the Gospels, from our knowledge of His Person as Son, we realize that everything Christ did or omitted was dictated by these two intentions. There is nothing solely for self. They were the ultimate cause of His thoughts and attitudes; in fact, we can conclude that His thoughts resulted from His one attitude toward His mission: "I have come to do

your will, O God.""¹¹ Finally, all of the virtues were and
are in His human soul in their fullness.

It is this interior life of the soul of our head that we
are primarily to reproduce and relive, especially His
sacrificial obedience to His Father's will, and the life
completely devoted to the Father of His risen state.
It is this interior life that we are to search out and study
in the Gospels and Epistles, and in the Old Testament,
especially in the psalms, which He used while on earth
as His own prayers, expressing His interior life.

We have treated briefly of Christ's interior. What of
His exterior life — His acts, sufferings, and words, what
spiritual writers call His mysteries? They direct us to
that aspect of His life which we have been considering,
for His "mysteries" are just what the word meant in its
early liturgical use: external realities that contain and
reveal a hidden content, which gives them meaning and
is transmitted through them. The external realities, like
the sacraments, are Christ's visible and audible acts, the
hidden content is twofold: His interior life and grace.
Cardinal de Bérulle wrote: ". . . the mysteries of Jesus
Christ are in a sense over, and in another sense they
continue and are present and perpetual. As far as execution is concerned they are over, but in their power they
are present and their power never passes, nor does the
love pass with which they were performed. . . . The
interior state of the exterior act, the efficacy and the
virtue that makes this mystery living and operative in
us . . . is *still living, actual and present to Jesus*.""¹²

¹¹ Hebr. 10:7.
¹² In Jean Gautier, S.S., *Some Schools of Catholic Spirituality*
(New York: Desclée Company, 1959), p. 309.

Exteriorly, then, Christ's mysteries are past; interiorly they are present, eternal, because the interior dispositions with which Christ performed them and the grace He merited by them are still present in Him. His birth is an historic event, but His intentions, His loving thoughts of the Father and of us, the virtues He exhibited, remain in His human soul. He merited the grace for us to make these thoughts and virtues our own, to have now the same interior that He had at His birth. We unite ourselves to this mystery, begging Him to give us these same dispositions. We are reliving His birth, or, rather, we are allowing Him to relive it in us, because He gives us the interior life that gave purpose to the exterior event. And so too with all His mysteries. From the analogy of head and body, it is logical that the rest of the body participates in the life the head lives. We are still "catching up" to the earthly life of our head. ". . . I am not yet perfected in Jesus Christ."[13]

"The phrase 'with Christ' is generally understood to mean a communion in his death and resurrection, which is not merely a relationship of similarity, but a real participation in the acts themselves."[14] But the interior life that informed all of His exterior acts is eternal, abiding now in the risen Christ. All the mysteries of the suffering, hence meritorious, period of His life are very much present in the risen Christ and in the Church in their action. We must "adhere" to them — the word is Bérulle's — i.e., we must unite ourselves to them by

[13] St. Ignatius, in *The Epistles of St. Clement of Rome and St. Ignatius of Antioch* (Westminster: The Newman Press, 1949), p. 61.

[14] Durrwell, *The Resurrection* (New York: Sheed and Ward, 1960), p. 221.

meditation and prayer, giving ourselves to Christ revealing His interior in them, that He might give us the
same aspect of His interior. He will do so by giving us
the grace merited by the acts to reproduce the virtues,
thoughts, and intentions so revealed, as well as, if possible, the particular acts. Our union with the death and
resurrection is, then, a union with His whole life. It
results in a co-operation: "with Christ."

We contact the mysteries of Christ in two sources:
the Bible and the liturgy. Christ's earthly life is present
in its eternal effects and in the interior life of His human soul in the sacraments, especially in the Eucharist
— Mass and Communion. We receive in Communion
the power for a union with Christ that is a oneness of
life, His life. A metabolism takes place, the reverse of
that which occurs in the case of ordinary food: we are
made into the food. We are feeding upon Christ's
mysteries. If we will they will take effect. ". . . at Holy
Communion the Christian's own personal union with
Christ is perfected so that his desires are transformed
into the desires of Christ, his sentiments into Christ's
sentiments, and therefore his prayer into Christ's prayer.
This, at least, is the effect to which the power of the
eucharist is ordained in . . . all the communicants."[15]

The Church presents certain mysteries to us in the
course of the year; these form the temporal cycle. They
are there for us in the feasts, seasons, and Sundays,
dynamic sources of Christ-likeness, to which we must
give ourselves that Christ might live.

---

[15] Conrad Pepler, O.P., *Sacramental Prayer* (St. Louis: B. Herder Book Co., 1959), p. 116.

What has been said here is of our obligation to relive Christ's earthly life, the acts of which are past. What of Christ's activity now? The Christian not only reproduces but also continues Christ's life. He is Christ visible and audible now. Christ still has work to do in the world, and, apart from coming visibly to earth again, or working moral miracles, He can only do it through us His members. He wills to contact others, to speak, to heal, to act. The Holy Spirit wills to give the benefits of Christ's priestly sacrifice. We must be a new human nature for Christ. The Word is made flesh in each member of His Mystical Body. We are, then, the extension and continuation of the Incarnation, Christ living in us and through us. We take Christ's place.

Spiritual writers use, besides the term *mysteries*, that of *states*, in relation to Christ's life. The latter are distinguished from the former in that they are abiding conditions, as, for example, a state of life. The chief states of Christ's life are His Sonship, His Incarnation, His state of victim (which includes His priesthood), and His risen life. Others are the various stages of His life: infancy, youth, manhood. Again there is Christ the teacher, the healer, the exorcist. The first four states we are all obliged to reproduce. As to the others, there is the matter of attraction and vocation. Some are won by Christ as an infant. This is with them a special devotion, and their spirituality consists in reproducing in themselves Christ's interior in this state. Thus He is reliving in them His infancy. As to vocation, Christ teaches, heals, and exorcises through those whom He has called not only to reproduce but also to continue these states. But all are obliged, as occasion offers, to continue these activities of Christ.

It may be objected that this spirituality would destroy our own personality. The answer is, yes and no. If Christ is to live, not I, everything in my character and personality that is opposed to Him must and will go. This is true and integral Christianity. We are united with Him primarily in the acts of His death and resurrection: death to sinful self and newness of life. On the other hand, Christ will make use of the good in me to contact others, especially those who would be more effectively won to Him only through me, through my gifts and my particular personality. Grace is founded on nature; it does not destroy it.

In reliving His life we are giving Him glory, for we are telling Him that each mystery is worthy of all praise. The Father is glorified because each act and word, each operation of His human intellect and will, were acts of love of the Father and service to Him, human nature pleasing the Father in the Person of the Son. And the life we are reliving and continuing is the perfection of the Father revealed in the Son. "But the life of His mystical body He wills to continue until the end of time in order to glorify His Father by the acts and sufferings of a mortal, suffering and laborious life, not only for the space of thirty-three years, but until the end of the world."[16]

Now we can better realize our end and our happiness, glory to the Father, through the Son, in the union of

---

[16] St. John Eudes, *op. cit.*, p. 5.

the Holy Spirit. Through and in Christ, as efficacious cause, we receive from the Holy Spirit the divine life, the virtues, the gifts, and actual grace. By the Spirit's activity, by Him as love joined to our love, we live with Christ, in a co-operation that results in ever greater glory to the Father as we more resemble the Son.

St. John's Gospel concludes with this sentence: "There are, however, many other things that Jesus did — so many that, should they all be recorded in full detail, the world is not likely to hold all the volumes that would have to be written."[17] We, the members of the Mystical Body, are the complete Gospel as we are the living Gospel. The Holy Spirit writes the life of our head in us and it will not be finished until He comes.

INDIVIDUAL ACTIVITIES

1. Meditate on the fact that your imitation of Christ is primarily an interior process: letting Christ live.
2. Concentrate in your gospel reading on the fact that in His earthly life and activities Christ was the image of the Father.
3. Meditate on the fact that continuing Christ's earthly life is giving glory to the Father and Himself.
4. For one day make your intentions those of Christ; on another, your attitudes; on another, your words; on another, your acts; and on the last, your omissions.
5. Study His words and acts to know His interior.
6. Think to yourself: "I take Christ's place," before each new activity.

---

[17] Jn. 21:25.

7. Give yourself totally to Christ in communion that He may live today. "*Et Verbum caro factum est.*"

8. Begin to search for Christ's interior in each feast of Christ and in each Sunday.

GROUP QUESTIONS AND ACTIVITIES

1. Discuss: Christ, rather than the saints, is your first and most necessary exemplar.

2. Discuss "exterior" and "interior" imitation of Christ.

3. Is "interior" imitation, letting Christ live, a passive process?

4. Discuss the fact that the exterior of Christ's mysteries is past, but their interior is eternal. How should this affect your celebration of the temporal cycle?

5. Why is it more important to relive Christ's interior than His exterior life?

6. Discuss the relation of Christ's interior with that of the Blessed Mother.

7. Discuss the value of taking Christ's place, letting Him live, for the apostolate.

8. Study the day's Gospel in order to understand Christ's interior.

CHAPTER 8

The Infused Virtues — Faith

What I hope to achieve: *To realize the position in my life of the infused virtues, and of the virtue of faith in particular.*

To synthesize the previous chapters: *The first seven chapters form the basic unit in this course, as is readily understandable from the past chapter. We may synthesize them in this way: our glory to God and our happiness are perfected through Christ (the divine life, virtues, and gifts), in Christ (the Mystical Body), and with Christ (reliving and continuing the Incarnation).*

At baptism God gives us sanctifying grace along with the infused virtues and the gifts of the Holy Spirit. These infused virtues are faith, hope, charity, prudence, temperance, fortitude, and justice. They are powers that give us the ability to perform supernatural acts.

We have been created in and through Christ on a supernatural level. Our end, which we can reach only through Christ our head, is glory to God in the beatific vision. Beginning with baptism we are united so closely with Christ that we are taken into the Trinity in a created manner. Our goal is to deepen this union throughout our life so that, at death, it may be perfected and sealed by the beatific vision. Everything in our life must be evaluated in terms of this glorious end. Our choices are determined by it. To maintain the high supernatural level to which God raised us at baptism we need supernatural power.

A virtue, in general, is a habit of good. Virtues are divided into natural and supernatural. The former have some natural perfection as their object, and the actions issuing from them are done out of a natural motive. For example, charity as a natural virtue is prompted by the good that one recognizes in another: one loves him because of that good, which, then, is the object and motive of such charity. We must not undervalue the natural virtues, especially those of honor, loyalty, trust, charity, candor, and courage. These perfect human nature, and grace is founded on nature, perfects it, and brings it up to the supernatural level.

Supernatural virtues, on the other hand, have God as their direct or indirect object and also as their direct motive. Supernatural charity, for instance, enables us to love God in another, because of His goodness seen in him. The supernatural virtues are increased with sanctifying grace, in the ways in which it is increased. They strengthen our natural powers and appetites, giving them the ability to perform supernatural acts. But the facility of virtue depends on our use of these supernatural powers; it comes with the repetition of acts of virtue.

We may have the power, but we don't have the habit of supernatural good until we put our power into operation habitually. If I have infused charity I am not necessarily charitable, but I do have the ability to be so.

The virtues of faith, hope, and charity are called theological virtues because God is their direct object and one of His attributes is their motive. These unite us directly to God.

The moral virtues of prudence, temperance, fortitude, and justice aid us to attain our supernatural end, the beatific vision, and the actions they elicit are done for a supernatural motive. They are means, helps, to practice the virtues of faith, hope, and charity.[1]

We shall consider the distinction between the seven gifts and the seven infused virtues in a later chapter. However, for clearness' sake, it is well that we understand now that the virtues act within us in a human manner, according to our human mode of acting, and that the operation of the gifts is strictly supra-human. For example, the virtue of faith gives us the ability to assent to revealed truth, but our knowledge of this truth is accomplished by the natural way of knowing — through the senses and the intellect, and our assent is given because of that which motivates the assent to any truth for which evidence is lacking, namely, authority, in this instance the authority of God. But when the gift of wisdom, the auxiliary of faith, operates, we experience God or knowledge of Him in our intellect in a quasi-experimental manner, which experience

---

[1] Cf. Adolphe Tanquerey, S.S., A Manual of Dogmatic Theology (Paris: Desclée Company, 1959), II, nos. 888–893.

strengthens our faith. In brief, the virtues give a supernatural direction to our powers of intellect and will,
which still must act in accordance with their nature.

Our supernatural life began with faith:

"What dost thou ask of the Church of God?" the
priest asked us at the threshold of the church.

"Faith," was our answer.

"What does Faith lead thee to?"

"Life everlasting" (Ritual for baptism).

Faith leads us to life everlasting because it gives us
the ability to believe in God and to assent to all the
truths He has revealed, because of His authority. God,
who is Truth, is the object and the motive of our faith.

Without faith, as we said in Chapter 1, we would
know God only as the conclusion to premises based on
rational observation. We would know Him only by
means of the image of His attributes seen in creation.
But ". . . what we believe by faith and what we see by
the beatific vision are one and the same thing . . ."
wrote St. John of the Cross.[2] Faith allows us, therefore,
to listen and assent to the knowledge of God that He
Himself has given us. Through revelation He has given
us glimpses of what He is in Himself. It is true that
now we see God as in a mirror, but it is, after all, a
reflection of God.[3] We don't understand the mystery
of the Trinity, but we do know the truth of God's life,
that it is the life of three Persons in one divine nature.
We don't understand the hypostatic union, but we do
know that Christ's human nature is possessed by the

---

[2] *Ascent of Mount Carmel*, Book II, Chap. 9.
[3] Cf. 1 Cor. 13:12.

Person of the Son. Faith also is a share of Christ's own knowledge of God. The knowledge that His divine nature gave to His human intellect He shares with us, His members, through faith, and this virtue in us honors His beatific knowledge, continues it, spreads its effects.

The object of faith is divine public revelation, which is found in Holy Scripture and Tradition, and is taught infallibly by the Church; it is the Word of God in the Church. We must assent to this Word with our intellect, but we cannot do so unless we are moved by our will. For this a special actual grace is necessary. Thus, we can see that faith is supernatural not only in its object and motive but also in its bestowal. The knowledge which this grace gives is entirely above our capabilities and beyond our meriting.

St. Thomas tells us that faith gives us certitude because of a "light" infused in our intellect by the Holy Spirit: "Three things lead us to believe in Christ; first, natural reason . . . secondly, the testimony of the law and the prophets . . . thirdly, the preaching of the Apostles; but when thus led we have reached belief; then we can say that we believe, not for any of the preceding motives, but solely because of the very Truth of God . . . to which we adhere firmly under the influence of an infused light; because faith has certitude from light divinely infused."[4]

Faith is the beginning and foundation of the supernatural life in us. ". . . so the Son of Man must needs be lifted up, that everyone who believes in him may

---

[4] In Garrigou-Lagrange, O.P., *Christian Perfection and Contemplation* (St. Louis: B. Herder Book Company, 1939), p. 67.

have eternal life."[5] We cannot enter the Trinity in the Son unless we believe in the Son and in all that He has revealed. Well does our request for faith take place at the church door, for faith is the door to our eternal duty and happiness of beatific glory. Faith was the fundamental virtue of the father of God's people: "Abraham believed the LORD, who credited the act to him as justice."[6] For us who know the Messia faith is necessary for our incorporation in Him.

Faith is necessary throughout our life in Christ during our time of trial. If faith gave initial significance to our supernatural end and to the means toward it, it must be ever present, living, and increasing, to give them significance now. Without faith now the beatific vision, sanctifying grace, and the Mystical Body mean nothing in our daily lives; they cease to motivate us, to influence our choices. They recede into a dim background from which they are taken from time to time, but they cease to be vital realities. Faith keeps love alive, as love keeps faith alive. Adam's trial was one of obedience. Ours is similar: faith. Once we yield to the forbidden fruit of disbelief, everything goes. The danger lies in the fact that we don't lose our faith, but that in practice we become unbelievers. It is necessary for us to have daily, living, faith to synthesize what we believe with our daily joys, duties, sufferings, and temptations.

The faith of an adult must be that of an *adult*. Fr. Voillaume has expressed this well: "Our manner of believing can hardly remain what it was when we were

---

[5] Jn. 3:14.   [6] Gen. 15:6.

seven. When we reach maturity, we naturally go through a spell of questioning, as I have said before, because we have to learn the divine truths over again with the intelligence of an adult. This is precisely what three quarters of the Christians fail to do today and their faith consequently remains the faith of a child in the wrong sense of the term — a puerile sort of faith too bound up with social traditions and sometimes tainted with superstition. They have not really tried to think things out."[7] This course is an opportunity to do this, and to apply dogma so realized as an adult to adult life.

We shall then see everything in our life with two sets of eyes: those of the body and those of faith. With the latter we shall pierce the exterior and see, in our sufferings, duties, and enjoyments, the will of Christ our head, desiring to live in us and thereby glorify His Father in us and through us. We shall see everything as a means to the beatific vision. This is the life of faith St. Paul writes of: "But my holy one shall live by faith."[8]

We must always remember that the truth to which faith is directed is invisible, and that we are living in a visible world. Faith appeals to none of the senses, whereas all around us is a creation that does. This is the reason why we must keep our faith alive in order to keep our love alive. Where do we find Christ visible, audible? In the Gospels, and there we must run to Him, living a while there with Him each day. If our life is to be Christ, visible, audible, He must be so to

---

[7] René Voillaume, in *Jesus Caritas*, January, 1960, p. 15.
[8] Hebr. 10:38.

us. We read the Gospels to know Him, to love Him, to live Him.

INDIVIDUAL PRACTICES

1. Are your choices determined by the beatific vision?
2. How much of your virtue is purely natural? with self as motive?
3. Meditate on the power you have to perform acts of the supernatural virtues.
4. Is your daily life founded on faith or self? Do you synthesize it with what you believe?
5. What in your life must be especially interpreted by faith?
6. Do you try to understand the why of what you believe?
7. Can you say that your own spirituality is based on dogma?

GROUP QUESTIONS AND PRACTICES

1. Discuss the difference between the natural and the supernatural moral virtues.
2. Discuss the fact that God is the motive of your faith.
3. Study the faith of Abraham. See also what St. Paul wrote of him in Romans 4. What was the object of faith in the Old Testament? Cf. Luke 24:25–27.
4. Discuss: Faith is a share in Christ's own knowledge of God.
5. Can you say that the forbidden fruit for you is disbelief?
6. How does one become an apostate? in the religious life?
7. What is meant by thinking out your faith? Isn't this doubting? How should we proceed in this?
8. Discuss: Authentic Christian spirituality is based on dogma.

CHAPTER 9

Hope

What I hope to achieve: *To appreciate the power of hope for my life.*
To synthesize the previous chapters: *Our glory to God and our happiness are fulfilled now and in the beatific vision through, in, and with Christ. Faith is our initial contact with Him and the condition of its continuance.*

Hope seems to be the neglected theological virtue, and yet it needs to be especially stressed in our times, when lack of goal and loss of confidence and courage cause so much mental illness.

Hope is the theological virtue that makes us expect with confidence the beatific vision and the means of attaining it, because of God's goodness and power. Its object is God, to be known and loved as He knows and loves Himself; its motive is God, for His goodness and power are God. "Having, therefore, been sanctified by faith, let us have peace with God through our Lord Jesus Christ, through whom also we have found entrance into this state of grace in which we now abide, and exult in the hope of participating in God's glory."[1]

[1] Rom. 5:1–2.

Hence by hope we expect our end and the means of attaining it. First among these means is the necessary grace. We are confident of receiving an increase of the divine life and actual grace in the Sacraments and through good works performed out of love of God. We shall consider actual grace later, but for the present it is sufficient for us to realize that it is a share in God's power. ". . . God is faithful and will not let you be tempted beyond your strength. On the contrary, he will, along with the temptation, supply you a way of escape, so that you will be able to hold your own."[2] It is also God's direction and His action, always with the beatific vision ultimately but clearly in view. We expect this help, and supernatural hope is this infused confidence.

Besides grace we need the other supernatural virtues and the gifts of the Holy Spirit. Hope helps us realize that these are ours, that if we co-operate they will do their work, that God will give their increase.

The circumstances of our life — our homes and families, parish, friends, school, talents, achievements — these are means to the beatific vision. Our religious community, its spirituality, work, houses, superiors and members, the novitiate itself with one's fellow novices, and the novice master, all of these are circumstances which Providence uses and will use to direct us to our supernatural end. Through hope we confidently expect the circumstances most perfectly adapted to preparing us for the beatific vision. Through hope we are certain of life "custom made" for us individually by God's will. Without these circumstances we might never reach the

---

[2] 1 Cor. 10:13.

beatific vision. And hope gives us the confidence that Divine Providence will make the best use of our past circumstances.

Related to the circumstances of our life are its trials, such things as sickness, death, failure, disappointments. These, too, are necessary, perhaps, if we are ever to attain the beatific vision, for without them we might lack that love of God that seems to grow only by trials. Of course, there are some persons so constituted that the trials in their life have to be few or relatively light. Through hope we expect the trials best adapted to our condition which will test and purify our love of God, which will detach us from self. "Not only this, but we exult in tribulations also, aware that tribulation produces endurance, and endurance proven virtue, and proven virtue hope."[3] We should note that our trials will not all be large ones, such as occur in major crises. They may be, but usually they are of the day-to-day variety, those proceeding from persons, employments, health, weather, dryness, monotony, restlessness, which are the very effective abrasives that grind away inordinate love of self.

Hope, then, is infused confidence that we are destined for the beatific vision, and that we will reach it, as far as God is concerned, and that we shall have all the helps we need to do this; that everything in our life, except sin and fault, is a means to perfect us for this vision, a means to union with God in this life. In this respect this confidence works closely with the "eyes of faith," which pierce the outer covering and see God's

---

[3] Rom. 5:3-4.

will within. Hope gives us confidence, perfect, blind trust in our loving Father, even when it *appears* that what He gives is not so loving at the time.

"And this hope does not disappoint, because God's love is poured forth in our hearts by the Holy Spirit who has been given us. While we were still helpless, Christ at the appointed time died for us wicked people. Why, it is only with difficulty that a person will die to save a good man. Yes, it is only for a worthy person that a man may, perhaps, have the courage to face death. But God proves his love for us, because when we were still sinners, Christ died for us."[4] Hope is also infused confidence in God's love for us. St. Paul's message is that God first loved us. His love of us is more important than our love of Him.

Hope gives us confidence in God's forgiveness because of His love and because of the infinite atoning sacrifice of Christ. *Christ* died for *us*.

Besides confidence, hope infuses courage into us. Weak and fearful, we are able, through hope, to face the difficulties in the spiritual life because "Our help is in the name of the Lord." Difficulties there are and will be, and our modern upbringing with its inventions and gadgets, geared to remove all hardships, has not conditioned us to undergo, let alone conquer, opposition to our self-will and self-indulgence. How we need this infused courage today. The very harshness of life, the inevitableness of work, prepared older generations for difficulties; now almost our only resource is grace and other supernatural helps, such as hope. It also gives us

---
[4] Rom. 5:5–8.

the courage to fight and to keep fighting, to "muddle through."

In an era when security is a people's noblest aim, conformity its means, and comfort its environment, mediocrity becomes its achievement. We have to battle this leveling-down process around us and aim at the highest in the spiritual order. Hope keeps our sights on the highest aim, the beatific vision, and makes us expect from God the best means. Mediocrity is really the fruit of fear and disordered desire; the superlative is the work of hope.

Hope is founded on God's revealed goodness and power. "And this is the sum of the eternal life — their knowing you, the only true God, and your ambassador, Jesus Christ."[5] The Preface for the feast of the Ascension tells us that where our Head is we also shall be. ". . . and, while they looked on, [He] was taken up into heaven, that He might grant unto us to be sharers in His own divinity." "But if we are children, we are heirs also; heirs indeed of God and joint heirs with Christ. . . ."[6] "By God's grace I am what I am, and the grace which entered me was not fruitless."[7]

When we pray, we must remember that God's concern with us is only with regard to the beatific vision. This may seem as if God is aloof from and indifferent to the little cares that mean so much to us, but this is not the case. He created us to give Him glory now and ultimately in the beatific vision, as well as to be

[5] Jn. 17:3.
[6] Rom. 8:17.
[7] 1 Cor. 15:10.

happy, which happiness consists in knowing and loving Him. Anything that is unrelated to these two ends is unworthy of God's consideration and of our own. If what we pray for is a means to the beatific vision, our request may be granted. If it is not, then we know that it is not the most effective means for us.

Since we should only pray for what is in consonance with our twofold end, we should be very careful that our prayer, even for material things, has this end in view. Hope, with faith, restores our Christian perspectives in this matter. Hope helps us to pray in Christ's name, which means praying as Christ prays, and hope accepts refusals from God as, at least for the time, better means to the beatific vision and our ultimate happiness than favors.

INDIVIDUAL PRACTICES

1. Once again see how everything in your day relates to the beatific vision.
2. See how everything in your day relates to happiness.
3. Know what are the real difficulties in your life. See how hope helps you through them.
4. Is your prayer always related to the beatific vision?
5. Meditate on the power of actual grace.
6. Meditate on the fact that God loved you first.
7. Realize the plight of a religious who has lost sight of the beatific vision as a determining factor.
8. See how the Rule and Constitutions are means to the beatific vision and to happiness.

GROUP QUESTIONS AND ACTIVITIES

1. How do your community works, your schools and hospitals, relate to hope?
2. Find quotations from the Gospels and Epistles relative to hope.
3. What is there in the Rule and Constitutions relative to this virtue?
4. What are the feasts of hope?
5. Relate the daily life of the novitiate to hope.
6. How can I teach this virtue to others after profession or ordination?
7. What are the future difficulties which can be solved by hope?
8. Give passages in the Psalms relative to hope.
9. Study the Ascension as the supreme glorification of Christ. Take texts such as John 17:5. Relate this glory of Christ to hope. You may profitably consult Dom E. Flicoteaux, O.S.B., *The Splendor of Pentecost* (Baltimore: Helicon Press, 1961).

CHAPTER 10

Natural Love

What I hope to achieve: *To realize that the essence of love is willing the other person as good, and willing his good.*

To synthesize the previous chapters: *We attain our end, glory to God now and in the beatific vision, and our own happiness now and eternally, through, in, and with Christ. Faith is our initial means of union with Him and with our end, and, together with hope, keeps Him and the beatific vision vividly in mind, and sees everything in our life except sin and fault as a means of giving God glory now and eternally.*

We approach with reverence the great virtue, the only eternal virtue, the one which supposes all the others, without which we are nothing! And because of its importance, its ramifications, and, too, misunderstandings as to its nature, we shall first study the natural basis for this supernatural gift. This basis is natural love.

What do we do when we love? With what human faculty do we love? It is important that we know the answers to these questions since we are only required to love.

When we love another we desire union with him because of some good we see in him. What happens is that our intellect presents this good to our will, and by means of the latter we choose the person as our good. This is the first step in love. There must be some desirable good in the other, which may range from moral perfection to some interest that we have in common. It stands to reason that the more enduring and noble is the good we see in another, the more enduring and noble will be our love for him. An ability to wear clothes well is hardly calculated by itself to inspire a lasting friendship.

Since this good is in the other person, we love not only this good in him but him because of it. We love him as the principle of his personality, character, and actions. We will him, therefore. This means that we go out to him in order to unite ourself to him. We may know good in someone, but love does not necessarily follow; love is only accomplished by our will.

Our first and basic instinct is the will to preserve and care for ourself. We will our own good. This good extends to our entire being. Hence, since our soul is the more important principle of our being, the good of our soul should be of greater concern to us. The next step in love is willing the loved one's good. We have already seen that there is good in him and that he is the root principle of that good. We have united ourselves to him by willing, by choosing him as good and this union has served to confirm our first conviction of his goodness. We then proceed to the permanent occupation of love. Presuming that what we love in the other is basically spiritual, hence abiding, we naturally will for the other whatever will foster that good and develop it, and we abhor whatever can harm that good. And the very "lovableness" of the other leads us to will his good always. Because our will is united to his in willing his good, we can conclude with a definition: love is the union of wills. When love is reciprocal it is perfect. Then his will is united with ours in willing our good; there is a true union of wills, united in their constant, unselfish activity.

The classic division of love is that into love of benevolence and love of concupiscence. The latter is, strictly speaking, not true love, for it wills the other person, not for his good, but for the selfish good of the one loving. It loves for the satisfaction, the pleasure, derived from the other. For example, John and Joe are friends, but John wants Joe as a friend primarily because Joe is generous with his money and his automobile, and is helpful in introducing John to influential people. Since there is a certain amount of give-and-take in any friendship, John has to reciprocate with favors to Joe from time to time, but these aren't given from love but only to keep Joe as a useful friend. This relationship on John's part is not a friendship because it is founded on the love of concupiscence, which, we can surely see, is not love at all. The same is true of a boy and girl who fancy they are "in love," when their "love" is based on the emotional and sexual enjoyment received from each other. We can realize by now how much so-called love, whether in friendships of expediency or in unwholesome romances, is not the real thing, and why it is basically important in the novitiate to understand what love is.

The love of benevolence is that which wills the other person's good for *his* sake. It is purely unselfish. We love even if the other makes no return, because we are not loving that he should make a return. We see him as good and we will his good. That is love. Such is the love of a parent for a child, whose own love is so often that of concupiscence. Such is the true love between a young couple, which, because of willing each other's good, conquers whatever would harm that good; which sees sharing the divine life as the highest good and effectively wills it for the other.[1] Such is the love of Father and Son, whose love is personified in the Holy Spirit. And the love of Christ for the Father was the pure love of benevolence. "May your will, not mine, be done."[2] "I am not seeking to do my own will, but the will of him whose ambassador I am."[3] The love of concupiscence loves in order to get; that of benevolence, in order to give. Charity, which is a Christian concept, is the love of benevolence supernaturalized.

Can both kinds of love exist together in a person? Yes, and they generally do. If that is true of our love for others we must note here that the love of benevolence must be uppermost and that we must be ready to sacrifice the love of concupiscence when there is any conflict between the two. The first should increase; the second, decrease. In practice, we should give to others, to their good, forgetful of self. Detachment from others

[1] Cf. 1 Cor. 13.
[2] Lk. 22:42.
[3] Jn. 5:30.

is in reality attachment to *them* and detachment from *self*.

But, from loving others, we know that love, although essentially the union of wills, also has an emotional element. This is not of the essence of love, but may accompany it because we are human beings whose nature includes both soul and body. It is unnatural to expect that we can love without the presence of the emotions, for our love must involve our entire being and personality. A good service which modern psychology has performed for the spiritual life has been to restore the body to its right relation to the spirit. Although the emotions or passions will be studied in more detail later on, we must here consider the emotion of love and its relation to love itself.

Emotions are psychophysical reactions, which, when vehement, are called passions. They are the result of fear or desire, or, to simplify, of love.[4] Images in the imagination and ideas in the intellect produce bodily effects, hence they lead to psychophysical reactions.[5] The heart is well chosen as a symbol of love because of the effect which the image of the one loved has on our heartbeat and blood pressure. The problems arising from the presence of the emotion of love may be expressed in terms of this symbol: the blood pressure is either too high or too low. There is either too much emotional content in our love, or too little. And if too little, do we really love?

---

[4] Cf. Adolphe Tanquerey, S.S., *The Spiritual Life*, no. 787.

[5] Cf. Narciso Irala, S.J., *Achieving Peace of Heart* (New York: Joseph F. Wagner, Inc., 1955), pp. 53–56.

As to the first problem: there is no better way to destroy love than to give a free hand to the emotion of love. The latter will always return to self and end by demanding from rather than giving to the other person. Uncontrolled emotion in general is always self-destructive. If the emotion of love is uncontrolled, it soon clouds our mind and blinds us to the good we see in the beloved. Ultimately, it obliterates this vision of another's good entirely, substituting for it the most specious good for self. Hence the emotion of love must be well controlled. It can be good and can be productive of great good. It can certainly help love along.

And that introduces the second problem: what about a love accompanied by little or no emotion? First of all, it *is* love, because there is the willing of the other's good. It is better to have this intention than to have the emotion without the essence of love. The union of wills accompanied by generally little emotion is the normal condition of love. For example, two people who have been married for some time do not, in their later years, have the strong emotional experiences which characterized their early years together. Yet the essential love, the union of wills, has developed, deepened. We can even say that true love will not develop unless the emotional responses lessen in their intensity. Without the aid of a strong emotion, we must, in order to keep giving unselfishly, love with the will alone. The effort to do so is very great, even super-human at times. But only in this way can love grow, can we prove that our love is truly love. The emotion is a help to love, but the test of true love is giving when this help is reduced or removed. This is the reason why our love of God continues and becomes strong, when our conduct is that recommended by St. Ignatius: "In time of desolation we must never make a change, but remain firm and constant in the resolutions and determination made on the day preceding this desolation, or in the preceding consolation."[6]

But what of the sexual drive in relation to love? Our contemporaries, in taking the former for the latter, have actually divorced the two, for when love is removed from the sexual drive there is no love. The true position of this instinct is in the service of marital love. It aids love, develops it, in the closest union possible between two persons, the state of matrimony, which state is its only favorable climate. Outside of matrimony there must always be this doubt: is the love of benevolence uppermost? The end of sex is the child. The image of the Blessed Virgin holding the infant Christ is a symbol and reminder that we as religious sublimate the sexual drive in spiritual parenthood.

Natural love is good. Not only is it natural to us, but necessary, and, to put it boldly, the most important, noblest, act of the natural man. But we have to reckon with a human nature weakened and disordered as a result of original sin. Therefore, we must follow rules which act as norms as to whether we are really loving. These rules will be given in the next chapter. For the present, check all love by this word, *give*. Spiritual writers inveigh against "particular friendships," and con-

---

[6] St. Ignatius Loyola, *The Spiritual Exercises* (London: Burns, Oates and Washbourne Ltd., 1952), no. 315.

fusion has sometimes resulted. We are not forbidden to love some more than others. Equal love for all is impossible and unnatural. Christ had His special friends, and part of the good He loved in Martha was her hospitality. What is forbidden is a friendship directed by emotion or the sexual drive, i.e., by *get* rather than *give*. Such an alliance is, of course, no friendship at all, for it is not based on love. Weigh all friendships against *give*. One in which the love of benevolence has concupiscence well and constantly under control is good.

Love is a necessity if we are to be human beings. With a will which naturally seeks good, which desires union with it, we would be frustrations and freaks of nature if we denied ourselves love. The condition of love is giving; its process, giving self away.

INDIVIDUAL PRACTICES

1. Recognize and appreciate the good in your companions.
2. Check the basis for your friendships. Do you esteem the spiritual good in your friends more than other "goods"?
3. Examine whether you love more with the love of benevolence than with that of concupiscence.
4. Examine the history of past friendships that failed to see whether failure was due to too much love of concupiscence.
5. Study a classic spiritual friendship between two saints.
6. Appreciate the love of benevolence of your parents for each other and for you.
7. Recognize the signs and approaches of a dangerous emotional friendship. What has to be done?

8. Add to your examination of conscience: "What did I give today?"

GROUP QUESTIONS AND ACTIVITIES

1. What are some of the "goods" which would form a basis for friendship? Which of these would make for lasting friendship?
2. A friendship that ceases to be never was a friendship. Discuss.
3. Is the pure love of benevolence between persons possible?
4. What is the role of emotional love in the spiritual life?
5. How can a religious be a spiritual parent?
6. What do the Rule and Constitutions prescribe about friendship? What do these passages mean?
7. What should be one's relations with the opposite sex?
8. Give a "character sketch" of an ideal friendship.

CHAPTER 11

Supernatural Love

What I hope to achieve: *To realize that my love of God is willing Him and His glory and that my supernatural love of others is loving Him in them, and them because of Him.*

Charity, we have said, is love supernaturalized. Even when divorced from a supernatural motive, the word still connotes the idea of giving. Here we shall only consider it as an infused virtue. It is defined as "a theological virtue that causes us to love God above all things, for His own sake, in the way in which He loves Himself, and to love the neighbor for God's sake."[1]

Since charity is supernaturalized love of benevolence, it consists essentially in willing God as good, as infinite good, for His sake. Through faith we realize that infinite good and God are synonymous. Because God is our good, the supreme object of our love, we will His good. But what is this? It can only be God Himself; therefore in this love of Him we will Him to be God, to be all the things, the attributes, He is. We will Him to be just, merciful, loving, all-powerful, all-

[1] Tanquerey, *The Spiritual Life*, no. 1210.

present, perfect. We will His glory, because He is His glory. Let us see an example of this. Suppose that we do something wrong and lawful authority punishes us for it. Since this authority, in meting out a just punishment, is sharing in God's justice, we will this punishment for ourselves, not only because we deserve it, but also because we will God's justice, which is Himself. We will Him to be just, we will Him to be God.

But in all God's treatment of us we discern His love, leading us to and preparing us for the beatific vision. And that is what He wills for us. He wills our good, which is the complete fulfillment of our entire being, especially of our intellect and will in beatific knowledge and love. Lesser goods there are, but we must always remember that God is the supreme good and the source of all good. And He has graced us with the undreamed-of favor of eventually uniting us to Himself. What matter the tragedies, disappointments, and sufferings, great and small, when we realize that in the way of a loving Providence these are means to the beatific vision, that God wills our real, not apparent, good.

The infused virtue of supernatural charity gives us the power to love God with the love of benevolence, to will His glory in all circumstances. The great comfort of the theological virtues is the fact that they are infused; they are poured-in abilities.

The object of charity is God in His totality, God with every attribute. Therefore charity must be founded on infused faith, on the knowledge of God which faith gives.

Charity is a love of Him "above all things." We do not say that we love God alone. This would be impossible. There are other lovable persons, who are lovable as themselves. But when there is a conflict, these lesser loves must yield to our one great love. We love God *first*, and ourself and everyone else *because* He wills us to. Thus we love Him *above* all others.

Although charity is the love of God "for His own sake," this does not mean that the love of concupiscence is necessarily excluded in an individual. However, the love of benevolence must predominate and be the deciding element in all conflicts. Thus De Guibert summarizes St. Bernard's four degrees of love in the following way:

"Man loves himself for his own sake and therefore wrongfully;

"Second, after conversion he loves God for his (man's) own sake, and not for Himself alone;

"Third, man loves God for Himself." (This degree is consequent upon the second, for familiarity with God gradually helps us realize His goodness and lovableness. Something similar occurs in our relations with others. For example, when we work with a very good person, we get to know him and, in time, come to love him. Love of benevolence is mixed with that of concupiscence in this degree.)

"Fourth, he loves himself solely for God's sake: but this last degree is that of the Blessed in Heaven, and St. Bernard does not know if it is ever perfectly attained by anyone in this life — 'Let those who have experienced this make such a statement; but as for myself, I must confess it seems impossible.' "[2] Tanquerey says this last degree is "attained by few in this life."[3]

If this fourth degree is pure love of benevolence, then we must conclude that the great majority of the perfect in this life are in the third degree, with, however, the love of benevolence predominating. The third degree admits of various stages, depending on the rising ascendancy of the love of benevolence. With this increase servile fear becomes more that of reverence, coupled with the operation of hope.

Just as faith is a sharing in God's knowledge of Himself, so charity is a sharing in God's love, "in the way in which He loves Himself." We are given the infused power to love as God loves; we have the ability to will Him, and this is the eternal operation of the Divine Will.

Love of neighbor through charity is not a separate virtue, but is one with the love of God. The infused virtue, then, includes both. When we love our neighbor with supernatural charity, we love God in him, and the motive of our love is the goodness of God. Hence, love of neighbor has the same object and motive as does love of God. In order to understand this, we must remember that a theological virtue has God as its object as well as motive.[4]

The lover looks for the beloved in everything and sees him in everything; everything reminds the lover

---

[2] Joseph De Guibert, S.J., *The Theology of the Spiritual Life* (New York: Sheed & Ward, 1953), p. 47.

[3] Tanquerey, *op. cit.*, no. 1217.

[4] This love also includes love of our neighbor himself, but only because of God, e.g., as a temple of God.

of his beloved. This is the principle underlying Christian love of neighbor. But we find God especially in man, the recipient not only of His image but also of His supernatural favors, especially the divine life, all of which have re-created man in God's likeness. We find Christ especially in man because he is at least a potential member of the whole Christ. Hence love of neighbor is the necessary effect of our love of God.

Thus supernatural love of neighbor, while it has for its object God seen in and through him, does not exclude love of the person himself, his good natural qualities, provided that what we love in him primarily is God, and that our love of him for himself is according to and because of God's will. Charity must be our fundamental mode of loving; it rules and may even inspire natural love.

What we love in our neighbor, then, is primarily God, the three Persons, dwelling in him through sanctifying grace, and Christ, his Head. "I tell you the plain truth, inasmuch as you did this to one of these least brethren of mine, you did it to me."[5] Frequently we think that constant charity toward our neighbor is impossible. However, when we see each one without exception as the temple of God and as another Christ, we realize that perfect, lasting love is not so impossible after all. How possible charity becomes when we understand that Christ's words include everyone. People cease to be merely people. We are surrounded by Christ.

Thus charity must be universal, extend to all. "Who is my neighbor?" Christ answered that question once

---

[5] Mt. 25:40.

and for all with His parable of the Good Samaritan. Our neighbor is everybody. If we exclude one person from our charity, we do not have charity, just as disbelieving one article of faith makes us a heretic.

Since in charity we see each one as Christ, what we do to others we do to Him. This will also prompt us to do. Everyone in need is Christ in need. Thus charity is the true motivation of the spiritual and corporal works of mercy.

Our words will be spoken to Christ present and about Christ absent. Seeing Christ in need of consolation or encouragement will prod us out of our self-absorption.

If we see Christ in our neighbor, we will refrain, when duty does not require it, from judging. All charity and uncharity proceed from thoughts, hence the basic need in this virtue to regard our neighbor with the eyes of faith. Forgiveness becomes easy then, for we cannot escape those inflexible words, "inasmuch as you did this to one of these least brethren of mine, you did it to me."

We shall desire for our neighbor all good according to God's will for him, as we would for Christ, and charity obliges us to carry out this desire by action as far as we are able. There are degrees of charity here, too, ranging from what we can do without seriously inconveniencing ourselves to the heroic charity that knows no inconvenience, that forgets self. "We know what love is from the fact that Jesus Christ laid down his life for us. We, too, ought to lay down our lives for our brothers."[6]

---

[6] 1 Jn. 3:16.

"A new commandment I give you: love one another; as I love you, so I want you, too, to love one another. By this token all the world must know that you are my disciples — by cherishing love for one another."[7] The charity of Christ is our criterion. But it is more; it is our charity, for He our Head is loving in and through us His members. We must remember that Christ wants to love *this person*, love him effectively, and we have the opportunity to let Him love through our love.

Our love of God does not exist without love of neighbor. "If a man boasts of loving God, while he hates his own brother, he is a liar. He has seen his brother and has no love for him; what love can he have for the God he has never seen? No, this is the divine command that has been given us; the man who loves God must be one who loves his brother as well."[8]

We go to God in and through our neighbor. He must not block our way. Hence some rules for safely and truly loving him must be given:

1. My love must be primarily giving, with no thought of return.

2. When there is a conflict, the love of benevolence must win out over the love of concupiscence.

3. This love must not be dangerous. Everything under control.

4. I must primarily love God in the other. There will be trials to test whether this is so.

The role of the Son in the Trinity is to please the

[7] Jn. 13:34–35.
[8] 1 Jn. 4:20–21.

Father, which He does by giving Him the twofold glory of being His image, and of loving Him. Now we better understand the meaning of the glory of the Son's love: He wills the Father as His good, as Father, the source of His being. He loves Himself, the being received from the Father. The Holy Spirit is this love. The infused virtue of charity enables us to love in this Trinitarian mode. The inner life of the Trinity is a mystery, its revelation is a grace. Hence, to love as Father and Son love is purely above our natural abilities. But we must remember that God has given us the power. To live as Christians we have to realize constantly that the infused virtues, especially that of charity, give us the ability to live, to love, as the Trinity lives and loves.

Our union with the Trinity and with all the members of the Mystical Body is perfected in Holy Communion. "He who eats my flesh and drinks my blood is united with me, and I am united with him."[9] "I in them and you in me. Thus their oneness will be perfected."[10] Communion is, therefore, the greatest means to develop supernatural charity, love of God and love of neighbor. The basic attitude toward this sacrament is that it is the sacrament of union. If love is the union of wills, Communion is the great opportunity in our day for Christ to give us His will, for us to give Him ours, and for all of His members to unite their wills in loving Him in each other. "For if we all partake of the one bread, we all become one body. Christ is

---

[9] Jn. 6:56.
[10] Jn. 17:23.

unwilling to be divided."[11]

Love is the only eternal virtue. When faith and hope will have led us to the beatific vision with the aid of temperance, prudence, justice, and fortitude, love will remain. In fact, eternity will be its great day.

INDIVIDUAL PRACTICES

1. Make an act of love of God based on what you have learned in this chapter.
2. Make an act of perfect contrition.
3. Make a collection of Scripture texts relative to charity. Memorize the most useful for recollection.
4. Make charity a point for particular examen.
5. Read St. John's First Epistle, after Communion.
6. Examine your love of God to see whether it is "above all things," whether in all your loves He holds the first place.
7. Examine your love of God to see whether it is predominately love of benevolence.
8. Examine your charity to others. Is anyone excluded? How must you proceed?
9. See how continuing Christ's charity makes our charity possible.

GROUP QUESTIONS AND ACTIVITIES

1. Discuss the fact that "I love you" is "I will you." Apply this to love of God.
2. Study the feast of and devotion to the Sacred Heart in the light of Chapters 10 and 11.

---

[11] St. Clement of Alexandria, Patrologia Graeca, 74, col. 560.

3. Discuss the fact that the love of Christ for us made His Passion and Death joyful to Him.

4. Discuss John 14:28 from the standpoint of your love of Christ with the love of benevolence.

5. Make a symposium on charity in the spiritual life of the Founder.

6. Collect short biographies of deceased members of the community who were noted for their charity.

7. What are the obstacles to community charity now?

8. Foresee the difficulties in the active apostolate.

CHAPTER 12

Charity — Obedience

What I hope to achieve: *To realize that obedience is charity, for it is the union of my will with God's as it comes to me through authority and the duties of my state in life.*

To synthesize the previous chapters: *My end is to give God glory in the beatific vision, and therein will be my eternal happiness. This supernatural favor was obtained for me through Christ's sacrifice. In Him I receive the divine life, and with Him I live a life of charity, founded on faith, supported by hope.*

Love is the union of wills. Love of God is union of our will with His. The question arises: how shall I know God's will? We receive God's will under two forms: the "signified will" and the "will of good pleasure." The first is His will as known to us in advance, the second, that which is unforeseen. In this chapter we shall consider only the former.

God's will as known to us in advance comes to us as the commandments, the evangelical counsels, the duties of our state in life, our religious Rules and Constitutions, the prescriptions of our vows, and the orders of our superiors. It is quite clear that these channels of God's will are foreseen, and although the substance and circumstances of superiors' orders may be unknown in advance, these orders are made in accordance with the Rule, Constitutions, and vows.

The special virtue whereby we respond to God's signified will is obedience. It is the union of our will with His when it comes to us in these foreseen media. Thus obedience is love, active love, and this is the only way we should view it. When obedience is equivalent merely to doing one's duty, to accomplishing a task, it is no longer a Christian virtue, and is by no means love of God. It may be good, even noble, but it is still a natural virtue.

The object of obedience is God's will, and its motive is God. The task imposed may be a very natural one, such as teaching English or working in a hospital, but the eyes of faith pierce the outer covering and see God's will within, and, therefore, Himself. And because this task is His will, we do it to the best of our ability. We take the most professional attitude we can. And we use the task as a means of that love of neighbor that would bring Christ to all and all to Him.

Civil authority is the lawful receiver and interpreter of God's will, as St. Paul tells us: "Let everyone submit himself to the ruling authorities, for there exists no authority not ordained by God. And that which exists has been constituted by God. Therefore, he who opposes such authority resists the ordinance of God, and they that resist bring condemnation on themselves."[1]

Church authority is obvious from Christ's words, "He who listens to you, listens to me, and he who despises you, despises me."[2]

Christ our Head speaks through His visible head, the Holy Father, and the bishops in the smaller "churches," the dioceses. The hierarchy of the Church gives the religious Rules and Constitutions, approves the superiors, and receives the vows.

Other forms of authority derive from the duties of one's state in life, such as those constituted by work, education, and lawful recreation.

The virtue of obedience demands that we not only obey but also unite our will with that of authority *because* it is God's will. Love is *willing* God's will. The perfection of the virtue would have us obey also the unexpressed but known wishes of authority in our regard, and St. Ignatius in his "Letter on Obedience" gives a final qualification, "He who would immolate himself totally to God must offer besides his will his intelligence also (which is the third and highest degree of obedience); so that he not only wills the same, but even thinks the same as the Superior."[3]

This is only possible if we see the superior as Christ. St. Benedict says simply of the Abbot, "For he is regarded as holding the place of Christ in the monastery. . . ."[4] And later St. Ignatius requires the same

---

[1] Rom. 13:1.

[2] Lk. 10:16.

[3] In *Thesaurus Spiritualis* (Bruges: Desclée De Brouwer, 1928), p. 433.

[4] *Holy Rule* (St. Meinrad: Abbey Press, 1937), p. 14.

viewpoint of the members of the Society: ". . . that you acknowledge Christ the Lord in every Superior, giving reverence and obedience with the utmost spirit of religion to the Divine Majesty in him."[5] Both legislators realize that in order to obey the superior as Christ we have to believe that Christ is directing us through him. We must never see our superior with the eyes of the body alone, but primarily with those of faith, since his dealings with us are primarily in matters which rest on faith. In fact, the less we view him as a man the better it is. In all that our superior commands, we should see Christ forming us for the beatific vision, enabling us to give the best and surest glory to the Father.

Dom Marmion comments on the third degree of humility in the *Holy Rule*[6] thus: "St. Benedict knows but one way of leading us to God; this is by union with Jesus Christ in His obedience."[7] Christ still wills to give the Father the glory of the obedience of His human will, and He does this through our obedience. "I have exalted thy glory on earth, by achieving the task which thou gavest me to do."[8] The most humble, obscure work is Christ working, obeying the Father's will in the obscurity, the "waste" of the many years at Nazareth. Besides, Christ's obedience was always directed to the redemption of men. His slightest act had a redemptive character. So our obedience, whether in some work

[5] *Thesaurus Spiritualis*, p. 431.
[6] *Holy Rule*, p. 30.
[7] *Christ the Ideal of the Monk* (St. Louis: B. Herder Co., 1926), p. 256.
[8] Jn. 17:4.

apparently unrelated to the apostolate or in one directly concerned with it, is Christ's obedience to the Father, willing Him to redeem mankind. St. Paul puts these words in the human intellect of Christ at the instant of His Incarnation, "See, my God, I am coming to do thy will."[9] Everything in His earthly life, His thoughts, words, acts, omissions, carried out this initial offering of Himself, this "good intention." These should be our words at the beginning of each day, a reminder that the Word is made flesh in us today, that it is *Christ* living His obedience in and through us today.

In the early stages of our religious life we are apt to think that union with God is essentially accomplished by prayer. We should distinguish: the union which is infused contemplation is the highest form of personal prayer, but in its essence union with God is possible only by means of the will. Infused contemplation is morally impossible if one's will is not already united with God's. Therefore union with God is love, the union of wills, and is, in practice as well as in its substance, obedience and abandonment. We do not have to retire into solitude or to a contemplative community for union with God. We have it now, here, in and by means of this task, this joy, this suffering. We may retire into solitude in the hope of a more favorable condition for infused contemplation, but not for union. And the Holy Spirit can and does give this purely supernatural prayer to those in more active communities. In the first sentence of the *Holy Rule* St. Benedict has stated the unitive character of obedience: ". . . that

---

[9] Hebr. 10:9. Cf. Ps. 39.

thou mayest return by the labor of obedience to Him
from Whom thou hast departed by the sloth of dis-
obedience."[10] There is no other way.

INDIVIDUAL PRACTICES

1. Read and pray Psalm 118 as relative to God's will.
2. Examine the motives for your obedience.
3. What are your weak spots in relation to this virtue?
4. Relate everything in your day to love. Each act an
   act of love.
5. Is your obedience solid love?
6. Meditate on Christ's obedience.
7. Make your prayer on waking, "Behold, I come to do
   Your will, my God."
8. Meditate on the fact that your obedience continues
   Christ's.

GROUP QUESTIONS AND ACTIVITIES

1. To what extent are the orders of superiors God's foreseen as well as His unforeseen will?
2. Take some work in the community and show how in
   spite of appearances it is God's will, how its secondary
   (apparent) object relates to that will, and how you
   would perform it.
3. Study the life of Abraham or one of the prophets as
   a study in fidelity to God's will.
4. Examine each item of novitiate life as God's will. What
   is God's purpose in each? How is each a means to the
   beatific vision?
5. What are the obstacles to obedience in the apostolate?
6. Why is love of God the highest form of glory?
7. Why is union with God achieved through the will?

---

[10] Holy Rule, p. 3.

CHAPTER 13

Charity — Abandonment

What I hope to achieve: *To realize that charity is the union of my will with God's in every moment.*
To synthesize the previous chapters: *I shall give glory to God now and in the beatific vision through Christ, in Him and with Him; now, founded on faith, supported by hope, accomplished by charity, the union of my will with His.*

God's "will of good pleasure" is His will with regard to events and conditions in our life that are not foreseen. Among such are sickness, death, afflictions, adversities, prosperity, consolations, and pleasures.

The union of our will with the signified will of God is the virtue of obedience; with the will of good pleasure it is the virtue of abandonment. A definition of this virtue is: conformity to the divine good pleasure, born of love, and carried to a high degree.[1]

In answer to the question asked in the past chapter, How shall I know what is God's will? We can conclude: God's will is everything in my life, my day, except sin

---

[1] Cf. Dom Vital Lehodey, O.C.R., *Holy Abandonment*. Also the article "Abandon" by M. Viller, S.J., and P. Pourrat, S.S., *Dictionnaire de Spiritualité*, Tome I, cols. 1–49.

and fault. It comes to me as the commandments, rules, orders of superiors, duties, and as the pleasant and unpleasant things which I can't foresee or be certain of. Though it wear a multiplicity of disguises I shall know it for God's will, for it is everything that is not sin or fault. "What treasures of grace are contained in each of these moments underneath the commonplace appearance of the events that fill them? Outwardly these events are no different from those which happen to everyone, but the interior invisible element discerned by faith is nothing less than God himself performing great works . . . the sacrament of the present moment! You present God in such lowly forms as the manger, the hay, and straw!"[2]

Faith sees God's will in its manifestation in the present moment, hope realizes it as a sure means to the beatific vision, and the will goes out to God, its good contained therein, in willing His will. Yes, in obedience and abandonment, our will must *will* what God wills for us, otherwise we wouldn't love. Love is the union of wills. Too often resignation is taken for this union, but resignation is imperfect and is by no means love. Rather it is self-love. It says in effect: God wills this setback for me. I don't will it, but I have to accept it because what else can I do? This is hardly the love of benevolence. Obedience and abandonment say: God wills this for me, *therefore* I will it too. Is this easy? Of course not, but it may become so. In some crises perhaps all we can say is: My God, I *want* to will Your will. If that is the very best we can do at the time, that is willing God's will, for He regards our sincere desire, hindered and confused by turbulent emotions as it may be. And He knows that in this condition we have the added advantage of being really humble without knowing it. If we can will God's will in a great affliction we may take pride in the fact. Wanting to will God's will is the same thing, but we feel we are such imperfect and unloving creatures because we can't seem to will it.

Abandonment is the perfection of obedience. If we were to stop with uniting our will to God's will as known in advance, i.e., to His signified will, and were to rebel against His will of good pleasure, we would miss the whole point of obedience, which is not to get a job done or to present a front of regularity, but to love. Obedience is one means to the practical love of God, abandonment is the other. We cannot love God sometimes or only in some of His manifestations. Love is total and eternal. Hence abandonment takes over where obedience leaves off. It responds to God's will when obedience stops because it is out of its territory. Abandonment makes sure we will God's whole will, all the time.

Yet, while abandonment is necessary for perfection, we must also have the virtue of obedience.[3] It does no good to will God's will in such things as sickness and adversity if we break the commandments or the Rule. Only those who are faithful to God's signified will and

---

[3] Cf. De Guibert, Theology of the Spiritual Life (New York: Sheed and Ward, 1953), p. 97.

will it under all its forms are more likely to be one with His will of good pleasure.

For a Christian, the specific motive for practicing the virtue of abandonment is the fact that Christ our Head did. We continue His earthly life, we take His place before the Father and before men. His initial sentiment, "Behold, I come, to do thy will" must be in us, must be ours. We continue the total union of His will with His Father's. "Not as I will, but as You will."[4] We are to relive not only His obedience but also His abandonment to the Father, evidenced by such circumstances as "the Son of Man has nowhere to lay his head."[5]

And the abandonment of the Mother of the whole Christ, how simply, heroically, and irrevocably was it expressed in her *Fiat*, "Let it be done to me." Mary's love for God is a perfect demonstration that love is obedience and abandonment. These two virtues were her guide in the difficult, because unprecedented, way she should proceed as mother of the incarnate God. Study the Gospels and see that this is so. Mary's spirituality consisted of obedience, abandonment, and recollection.

The providence of God is another motive for abandonment.[6] Divine providence is God directing us to the beatific vision by means adapted to us individually. God knows from eternity what each one of us needs. He knows, for example, that if we continue in this work,

---

4 Mt. 26:39.

5 Mt. 8:21 (Conf. ed.).

6 Cf. Tanquerey, *A Manual of Dogmatic Theology,* I, no. 511.

this place, or with this person, we shall be damned. What looks like the end of our world is in reality the safeguard of our eternity. *Omnia cooperantur in bonum,* "All things work together for good to those who love God. . . ."[7]

What we have to do to practice abandonment is to will God's will in the present moment. This is not always easy, but it is simple. We are not careless about the past and future; we try to repair past mistakes and negligences and prudently provide for the future. But as for anxiety about either, we leave the past to God's mercy and the future to His providence.

When we are conscious of continually doing and accepting God's will, whether in obedience or abandonment, we simplify our whole life. Instead of doing a multiplicity of actions, we come to realize that we are doing one thing. Eventually, if someone were to ask us at any point of our day what we were doing, we would not reply, "I'm recreating," "I'm working," "I'm praying," but "I'm doing God's will." His will comes to us under many appearances, in many disguises, but we know that all day long there is only one thing. And where God's will is, there is God because He is simple. Our spiritual life must be as simple as God; it must be in His image.

What is the purpose of God's will in our regard? What is the purpose of life? Glory, glory, glory. That we might give Him glory in the beatific vision, and now, in our time of trial and formation for this end. Our happiness, now and eternal, is relative to the bea-

---
[7] Rom. 8:28 (Conf. ed.).

tific vision. And since the Father receives perfect glory from the Son, His will is to make us into Christ.

When young religious leave the clericate after ordination, the novitiate or juniorate for the works of the apostolate, they notice that they have less time for religious exercises than they did previously; silence is not so great, their work is long and absorbing. They miss the conferences which might give meaning to the changed circumstances. As a result they feel that union with God in such a life is impossible. Remember what was said in the past chapter; union with God is accomplished by means of the will. This means, in practice, that we achieve this union by means of the virtues of obedience and abandonment. "The state of divine union consists in the total transformation of the will into the will of God, in such a way that every movement of the will shall be always the movement of the will of God only. . . ."[8] The end of union with God is not our enjoyment, but *His*. We unite our will with His so that the Father might make us into the One in whom He is well pleased. If we can give Him the glory of being another Christ, love should make us happy. Abbot Butler has wisely written concerning union with God: "We have had it on the authority of St. Teresa and St. Alphonsus, and of St. Benedict before them, that perfect love of God, a perfect union with Him, may be attained by entire renunciation of our own will, and perfect conformity to God's Will, and this without the mystic union. And the same seems to be Our

[8] St. John of the Cross, *The Mystical Doctrine of St. John of the Cross* (New York: Sheed & Ward, 1935), p. 13.

Lord's lesson in the Gospels."[9]

Love is giving. Our love of God is giving ourself to Jesus that He might live, not we. Our Trinitarian love must be that of the Son, who gives Himself, without any reservation of self, to the Father. Love is achieved by means of the will: only by our will can we give ourself and our life to another. So by the virtues of obedience and abandonment we give ourselves to the Father in Christ. Only by these virtues do we truly love.

INDIVIDUAL PRACTICES

1. Meditate on the various appearances God's will takes in the course of one day.
2. Make this the basis for recollection.
3. Examine yourself on your *willing* God's will in sufferings and adversities.
4. Meditate on the abandonment of Christ, your Blessed Mother, St. Joseph, your Founder.
5. Meditate on the advantage of the doctrine and practice of abandonment in your relations with difficult persons.
6. Offer the Mass in the spirit of abandonment.
7. Foresee difficulties in the apostolate and relate them to the virtue of abandonment.
8. Relate abandonment to mental health; to neuroses.

GROUP QUESTIONS AND ACTIVITIES

1. Discuss: Does God will sin and fault?

---

[9] Dom Cuthbert Butler, O.S.B., *Western Mysticism* (London: E. P. Dutton & Co., Inc., 1951), p. lvi.

2. Prepare a symposium on abandonment in the lives of certain selected saints.

3. How does abandonment simplify your life?

4. In abandonment you are continuing the union of Christ's will with the Father's. Is it also union with Christ's will with regard to the apostolate?

5. Why does the agony in the Garden of Gethsemani exemplify the abandonment of Christ?

6. Give other examples from His whole earthly life of Christ's abandonment.

7. Defend the fact that union with God consists essentially in the virtues of obedience and abandonment rather than in prayer.

CHAPTER 14

Charity — Zeal

What I hope to achieve: *To realize that charity results in zeal.*

To synthesize the previous chapters: *My glory to the Father now and in the beatific vision will consist in my being for Him another Christ. This will be accomplished by the union of my will with His, through, in, and with Christ, in the virtues of obedience and abandonment.*

"Charity's most sublime expression is the apostolate, whereby the Christian not only knows, loves and serves the Lord completely and fervently but dedicates himself to making Him known, loved and served."[1] These are the words of the founder of a secular institute, that new form of the life of perfection in the Church, in which the members bring Christ to the most unlikely persons and places.

Zeal is the natural flowering of love. It is the intense desire to make others love God. This desire follows from the nature of the true love of benevolence. When we recognize good in another we want others to do

[1] Giovanni Rossi, *This Way to God* (Morristown: Villa Walsh Press, 1954), p. 190.

the same. We want them to give glory to the one loved
by an acknowledgment similar to our own. How many
young men have bored their friends with the picture
of their beloved, waiting anxiously for some word of
admiration for her beauty?

How much more do we want others to know, love,
and give glory to God once we love Him. And God,
who is infinite Good, our all-absorbing, all-consuming
love, sends us out into the highways and byways, com-
pelling everyone to love what we love. Especially is this
the case when we are convinced that He has first loved
us, when we are struck with the proof of this, and
the manner of the proof: "God's love was made manifest among us by the fact that God sent his only-
begotten Son into the world that we might have life
through him. This love consists not in our having loved
God but in his having loved us and his having sent
his Son as a propitiation for our sins."[2] God loves us,
the Father loves us in Christ. We love in return, and,
like the Apostles at Pentecost, filled with the Spirit of
Love, rush to tell the "good news," that here is the
true Good, that all must return the glory of love to
proven love. This is zeal. This is what compels us after
ordination or profession to go into the harvest fields
and what keeps us going year after year, task after task.
Not the love of action, variety, enjoyment, or ambition,
but the desire to bring others to love the One we love,
and to love Him as we do.

Zeal proceeds from love and leads back to love. There
is no fundamental clash between them. There is no

---

[2] 1 Jn. 4:9–10.

clash between contemplation and action when each is true. Both are aspects of the same act — love. Just as writing a term paper is a single "action" comprising a number of operations, so is love. We go to prayer out of love, and we go to action impelled by that same love.

The dichotomy between action and contemplation results from a dichotomy between action and being: action is not related to being. For example, a priest-religious is assigned to coach a high school basketball team because he knows the game well. He coaches it and has a successful season, but throughout he feels that action is a long way from contemplation, that coaching is not conducive to his spiritual life. His trouble is that he has divorced action from being. He was given the job not only because he had the ability to be a good coach but also, and mainly, because he was a religious, a man who loves God first, who should see the job as God's will. His state of being is fundamentally not that of a coach but that of an intense lover of God. The action that results, coaching, is only the result of his state of being. It is only when a religious loses sight of his essential being that "good works" can lead him astray. Action that follows love is a form of love.

Zeal is to give to others what we have learned in contemplation, which is the program of the Dominican Order. We cannot give what we don't possess. When our spiritual life, our love of God, is intense, when we realize at the beginning of and all through our day that we take Christ's place, with His attitudes, words, acts, then we have something to give. "He who abides in me, and I in him, he bears much fruit."[3]

Zeal is witnessing to Christ. "And you, too, will witness, because you have been with me from the beginning."[4] Our lives, for example, are living proof that Christ is God, that Christianity is true. Our words, our teaching, are evidence that we not only know about Christ but that we speak "what we have heard, what we have seen with our own eyes, what we have gazed upon, and what we have embraced with our own hands."[5] We are witnesses because we were there. We were with Him this morning in the Sacrifice, in Communion, in the Gospels.

"Zeal will only get results in so far as it is united to the action of Christ Himself."[6] In all of our apostolic works we must remember that it is primarily Christ our Head acting through us His members. In our love of Him we give Him our humanity completely that He may continue to "cast fire upon the earth"[7] through our contact.

Thus through zeal we ourselves become spiritual parents of those whom we bring into the Mystical Body. Everyone in whom we have planted the seed of the Word becomes our child. We may only sow and another reap, but the fruits will also be ours. Of course this means that the grain that is ourself must die to self and its constant demands if we are not to go to our graves alone.

---

[3] Jn. 15:5 (Conf. ed.).
[4] Jn. 15:27.
[5] 1 Jn. 1:1.
[6] Dom Chautard, *The Soul of the Apostolate* (Trappist: Gethsemani Abbey, 1946), p. 192.
[7] Lk. 12:49.

What is the measure of our zeal? St. Paul gives us our rule: "But I will most gladly spend myself and be spent to the limit, for the sake of your souls, even though the more I love you the less I am loved."[8] There is no measure then; zeal is boundless, and its works are without limits. There is no place here for the professionalism that limits zeal to office hours. While we may have to maintain such devices for efficiency and balance, zeal does not stop when we leave our office.

Opposed to zeal is self-seeking, as we shall experience. It will be much more attractive to watch television in the rectory on a Saturday evening than to spend those hours in the confessional; it will be more enjoyable to close our door and settle down with a good book than to open it to needy persons. And when we do perform apostolic works, self may intrude to such an extent that we are only waiting for them to be over so that we can recreate ourselves. Father Lallemant's advice is very valuable here: "If in our employments we practice the exterior of virtue without the interior, we are miserable, bearing the weight of exterior labour, but never tasting interior unction and sweetness; and this makes us fall often into notable faults; whereas by means of recollection and prayer, we should effect more in our ministrations with less difficulty, weariness, and danger, and with more perfection to ourselves, more advantage to our neighbor, and more glory to God."[9]

We must have the zeal of St. Paul, preaching in

---

[8] 2 Cor. 12:15.

[9] Père Lallemant, *Spiritual Doctrine* (Westminster: Newman Book Shop, 1946), p. 190.

season and out of season the saving word that we are sons of God, that the divine life which we receive in the risen Christ transcends the difficulties and sorrows of our human life, that in the victory of Christ we are victorious over sin.

INDIVIDUAL PRACTICES

1. Examine yourself on your zeal.
2. See how simple, ordinary charity to neighbor can be also the result of zeal and have the same effect.
3. Look through one of the Gospels and find evidence of Christ's zeal.
4. Study the "Propers" of the feast-day Masses of some of the saints noted for their zeal.
5. Read the portions of the Rule and Constitutions relative to zeal and the community works.
6. Engrave this deeply in your soul through meditation, recollection, and practice: *I take Christ's place.*
7. Collect New Testament texts on the fact that you are witnesses to Christ.
8. Foresee the fight between zeal and self that will constantly take place during your apostolate.

GROUP QUESTIONS AND ACTIVITIES

1. Discuss the good and bad points connected with the works of the community and how zeal is related to both.
2. What makes zeal grow cold?
3. Discuss: There is no dichotomy between contemplation and action.

4. Discuss the fact of spiritual parenthood of priest and religious. How is this done?
5. Discuss professionalism vs. zeal.
6. What are the enemies of zeal in the apostolate? in various works? at different ages?
7. What is "the heresy of good works"?

CHAPTER 15

Charity — Related Virtues

What I hope to achieve: *To realize some of the practical implications of the virtue of charity to my neighbor.*
To synthesize the previous chapters: *My glory to the Father now and in the beatific vision will consist in my being for Him another Christ. This will be accomplished by uniting my will with His, through, in, and with Christ. My love of God will result in zeal to bring others to this love, this end.*

There are three practical expressions of charity to our neighbor that we shall consider in this chapter: affability, adaptability, and accessibility. Much of the material on these has been taken from the *Maryknoll Spiritual Directory* by Bishop James E. Walsh, a book that should be read by all during the novitiate.

Affability is a pleasantness of manner, a cheerfulness with others, and a manifest happiness to be in their company. This happiness shows in our facial expression, our words, our actions, and, far from being the kind of thing calculated to "win friends and influence people," is rooted in a supernatural, and, as far as possible, natural love of them. "The affability of the missioner is a refinement of charity by which he puts aside his own self-interest in order to be interested in others."[1]

Because of charity we owe affability to every member of the community. What does this mean? It means that we must be genuinely interested in each one; hence, we must know them and know about them, their interests, accomplishments, sorrows. A big task? Yes, but so is charity. And what is practical charity if it doesn't demand and obtain such an interest in others? Consuming? Yes, but isn't charity giving self away? Since natural love begins with like, such an interest will discover something to like even in those whom we may dislike now. This interest is accompanied by a happiness to be with others and a corresponding pleasantness. We must be cheerful and charming and warm, not with a sentimental warmth, but with a genuine affection that we are not afraid to show.

St. Francis de Sales, that master of affability, tells his Visitandines, "Let them not bring to recreation a sad and morose countenance, but let their face be pleasant and affable; and their conversation be such as the Constitutions describe."[2] And the passage from the Constitutions: "The sisters shall keep together at recreation and while they are at work, shall converse on some agreeable subject, in a pious and cheerful

[1] Bishop James E. Walsh, Maryknoll Spiritual Directory (New York: Field Afar Press, 1947), p. 67.

[2] Spiritual Directory for the Sisters of the Visitation (Roehampton: Manresa Press, 1930), p. 292.

strain, with peace, sweetness, and simplicity."³ How
many later Constitutions have echoed these words. And
yet we remain absorbed in self, in our own aches, disappointments, work, and interests, and when we speak
it is to murmur or complain. Two spiritual attitudes
that must be cultivated by members of a recently
founded secular institute are:

"Refrain from interior or exterior criticism to prove
that she loves the environment in which God wants her
to sanctify herself.

"Refrain from interior or exterior complaint to show
God she loves the form in which He presents Himself."⁴

Affability is an essential in the apostolate. "In practice this means he [the missioner] puts aside his own
comfort and convenience, prerogatives and prepossess-
sions, time and trouble, in order to be of service to
others. Affability is a feature of zeal, a sign of charity,
and an essential of true spirituality in a good missioner.
. . . He also knows that he cannot attract anybody
unless he makes himself attractive to people by a generous and whole-souled affability."⁵ The people whom
we contact will soon enough "get our number." They
will know whether the great love of our life is God or
self, and they will not be attracted for too long by
the latter. And a false affability, one proceeding from
love of self, will not hold up for long either.

Let us study the affability of Christ, for it is His

³ *Constitutions of the Sisters of the Visitation* (Roehampton:
Manresa Press, 1930), p. 115.

⁴ From material supplied by the Oblate Missionaries of Mary
Immaculate, Cap-de-la-Madeleine, P.Q.

⁵ Walsh, *op. cit.*, pp. 67–68.

affability we are to continue. How this quality must have radiated in Him when He called the Apostles, how constant it was in all His conduct with them and the disciples. We see evidence of it in His manner with the ordinary crowds, as, for example, the group which raced Him to the other side of the lake when He wanted a little solitude.[6] It was not always healing they wanted; at times they simply wished His teaching and presence. But it is in the risen Christ that we observe an almost playful affability, as on the way to Emmaus, and the risen Christ is especially our ideal. In all of this we learn that Christ's affability is the result of His utter selflessness, of the union of His will with the Father's, for His glory and man's redemption.

We can conclude this section on affability in no better way than to repeat the words of St. Francis of Assisi on joy: "Always, my beloved Brethren, have a holy joy in God, both interior and exterior. If the servant of God endeavors to have and to keep spiritual joy, which springs from a pure heart, and is acquired by devout prayer, then the devils cannot harm him. . . . Sadness belongs to the devil, and his children, but to us perpetual joy and jubilation in the Lord."[7]

Adaptability is charity when it is the adjustment of self to every person and circumstance coming to us by way of God's will. "Man is a creature of habit, and this law of his nature is at once a salutary help and distinct danger. Good habits aid us greatly in the cor-

---

[6] Mk. 6:30–45.

[7] *Works of the Seraphic Father St. Francis of Assisi* (London: R. Washbourne, 1890), pp. 115–116.

rect reactions to given situations; and similarly, bad habits make it doubly hard to counteract bad tendencies in accordance with spiritual principles and ideals. . . . For the missioner, however, the elimination of bad habits is not enough. In his case there lurks an additional danger in the formation of good habits, because the conditions he must face on the field will often require a departure from his customary way of acting even when his habit is in itself commendable. It is a good habit to anticipate the recitation of the Divine Office, but adaptability must interpose to vary this habit at times when there is a more peremptory demand made upon one's time by charity or some other urgent duty. . . . Our vocation is to preach the Gospel and to save souls, and all our duties, spiritual or otherwise, must be regulated so as to contribute to this great end and not to interfere with it. While being grounded in spiritual principles that never fluctuate, the missioner must also incorporate in his character formation a certain flexibility by which his habits and routine duties are readily and efficiently adjusted to the circumstances of his work."[8]

Bishop Walsh is writing here of the extreme circumstances of mission life, yet his message fits those of the ordinary apostolate as well as day-to-day community life. There must be regularity in our lives, because it is God's will that we be regular. But regularity must also yield to God's manifest will. Regularity and routine are not ends; they may even be maintained out of pride. We have to be ready for God's will under any form.

[8] Walsh, *op. cit.*, p. 59.

Beware of developing into an "old maid." An "old maid" may be male or female, single or married. The term does not represent a state of life but rather a state of soul, characterized by an absorption in self and a magnifying of the petty. And because his little routine looms as important in his eyes, the "old maid" will not break it or bend it. Many a religious slowly becomes an "old maid," beginning with the overabsorption of the novice in his spiritual life and ending in the self-and-comfort-seeking of middle age. Remember what our spiritual life is in essence: love of God, who is within us and outside of us, who is loved in every person and in everything in which we discern His will.

Accessibility then follows from the preceding. We must let Christ be accessible to all those He wishes to contact through us. We have no time for self. There is time for legitimate recreation, of course, but only when this is taken as re-creating ourselves for more intense union with Him and for the apostolate. And even when we "come away into a quiet place and rest awhile" He comes with us. See the accessibility of Christ. Crowds, always crowds. And His way of healing them is so often by touch, contact. So today crowds still need this touch of Christ, are clamoring to be healed, and they can only come to Him through our being accessible.

We conclude the chapters on charity with a brief consideration of perfection and purity of heart. Christian perfection is love of God when such love is a perfect union of our will with His. This love is given God in, with, and through Christ and attains its end in the eternal love of the beatific vision. Since the natural perfection of a man consists in the perfect exercise of his highest faculties and in his attaining his end, it is obvious that on the supernatural level both of these criteria of perfection are completely satisfied. To know infinite Truth is not enough. That is theory alone.

When Truth is presented to the will as Good, theory leads to practice or, rather, to the union that the will desires and for which it was made. Love unites the whole person to God; nothing is left out. "It lays hold of our entire soul, intellect, heart, will, activity, and delivers all unreservedly to God."[9] Love comprises all the virtues, not in the sense that it substitutes for them, but in the sense that its perfection supposes them. And finally, love is the perfection and crown of all the virtues. Without it there can be no true virtue.

We shall treat of purity of heart in a later chapter. But its relation to love must be stated here as a final word on the great virtue. Purity means oneness. Pure gold is one substance. Purity of heart is one love. This does not mean that we love God alone, but it does mean that we love Him first, with the primacy that would destroy every conflicting love. Chastity must only be viewed in this regard. Our vow of chastity requires us to have a pure heart, one love. There is no room in our heart for a love that disputes or usurps this love or that is loved for itself, apart from it. Purity of heart, then, is the result of love. The way to chastity is this all-consuming love of God.

---

[9] Tanquerey, *The Spiritual Life*, no. 317. Cf. nos. 316–319.

INDIVIDUAL PRACTICES

1. In the Gospels look for evidence of Christ's affability and accessibility.
2. Examine your interest in others, all others, in the community.
3. Resolve never to criticize or complain.
4. Resolve at recreation to recreate others.
5. Examine your motives for regularity.
6. Examine self for evidences of "old maidiness."
7. A good resolution: never judge superiors, equals, or inferiors, unless your office obliges you to.
8. Examine your purity of heart.
9. Are you a means to Christ for others? or an obstacle?

GROUP QUESTIONS AND ACTIVITIES

1. Discuss the relation between affability, charm, "personality," and popularity, and the uses and dangers of each in the apostolate.
2. Prepare a symposium on deceased members of the community who were outstanding examples of these three related virtues.
3. Conduct a recreation in which no one is allowed to use the first-person pronoun or pronominal adjectives.
4. For a determined period penalize anyone who complains or criticizes.
5. What did Pius XII mean by adaptability for religious?
6. Conduct a "chapter of faults" in which each one accuses himself of his "old maidiness."
7. Discuss the process whereby a religious can become and remain an "old maid."
8. Discuss: perfection is the perfection of love rather than the acquisition of all the virtues.

CHAPTER 16

Formal Prayer

What I hope to achieve: *To realize that prayer is the communication of love and to value liturgical and community prayer in particular.*

Union with God is accomplished by means of the will. To quote St. John of the Cross: "The state of divine union consists in the total transformation of the will into the will of God. . . ."[1] Essentially this is effected through the virtues of obedience and abandonment, without which union is impossible. But this is not enough, it does not completely satisfy, in fact, it would not endure for long without that other means of union, prayer. One of Dom Augustine Baker's definitions of prayer is "a desire and intention to aspire to a union of spirit with Him."[2] Prayer is basically the desire for union with God, an effective desire. That is our reason for stating that without prayer the union of our will with God's would not last. It is preceded, accompanied, and sustained by the *desire* for union.

---

[1] St. John of the Cross, *op. cit.*, p. 13.

[2] Augustine Baker, O.S.B., *Holy Wisdom* (New York: Harper and Brothers, n.d.), p. 342.

And, of course, without this desire for God what glory to God or happiness is there for us in such a union?

"Take away desire," writes Père Sertillanges, "the prayer ceases; alter it, the prayer changes; increase or diminish its intensity, the prayer soars upward or has no wings. Inversely, take away the expression while leaving the desire, and the prayer in many ways remains intact."[3] Thus it becomes possible to obey St. Paul's words, "never cease praying."[4]

Prayer, essentially the desire for God, seeks union in every possible way. But its own proper way is through the intellect. The intellect may be absorbed by the task imposed by God's will, but desire makes it look for the first opportunity to rest in Him. The intellect's joy is the thought of God, and the thought flames the desire for Him, the love of Him. Love goes out to Him, will to will, and leads back to the loving thought when there is again opportunity. It is a cycle, the eternal cycle of our activity in the beatific vision begun now.

Prayer then is the communication of love, communication in the sense of two intellects communing, a telepathy. But it is not a mere telepathy of ideas or images, but one in which thought is presence of the One loved and love the consequence. Let us stop thinking of prayer as words, forms, exercises. Whatever Rules and schedules have to call it, prayer is either the desire of and communication with God, or it is nothing much.

---

[3] A. D. Sertillanges, O.P., *The Intellectual Life* (Westminster: The Newman Press, 1959), pp. 69–70.

[4] 1 Thess. 5:16.

Prayer doesn't need words, since it is whole and intact as a loving thought, a desiring thought. Words may help thought and desire, they in their turn break into words, but words are not the essence of prayer.

As to form, we may divide prayer into that which is either formal or spontaneous. The former is a set "formula" of words, such as the prayers of the liturgy, our community prayers, and all previously composed prayers. The latter is just what the term denotes, spontaneous, springing from the grace of the moment. It may be silent or vocal, expressed in a thought, an image or words.

The matter or substance of prayer is God. If it were not, how could it still be considered as a loving, desiring thought of Him? Perhaps that is what has been wrong with our prayer: its substance has been self. For example, the prayer of petition is a good prayer, highly commended by tradition. What should we be asking of God in this prayer? The beatific vision. Oh, yes, we may be asking Him for a change of occupation, but it isn't really that that should ultimately interest us. The true prayer of petition asks that, if a change of occupation will in God's eternal knowledge be a more effective means for us to the beatific vision, He grant it to us. Haven't we rather prayed something like this: My God, please grant me a change of occupation? Of course, we added, if it is Your will, but did we really mean this? And if He didn't grant us our favor would we be willing to will His will?

The substance of prayer is God; whether we praise, adore, thank, beg pardon, love, or petition, the ultimate subject matter is God, because prayer is a communication of love. In the beginning praying in this manner may not be easy. We may have years of a rather self-centered spirituality to undo, but now is the time to correct, to relearn, to reorientate. If our spirituality is to be founded on a rock, we must learn to pray truly. When Christ taught His novices to pray He first orientated them toward God.

Another matter we must realize well: work is not prayer. How can it be if prayer is a loving *thought* of God? How can, say, teaching, which demands concentration on subject matter as well as on classroom discipline, be a thought of God? It may and must be interwoven with prayer, albeit very brief, but in itself it is work. So we must not lull our consciences that much activity is going to substitute for prayer because the good intention "makes everything a prayer." The good intention does not. It makes everything meritorious and consecrated to God out of love, but we're still going to have to pray. We shall take this up in the chapter on recollection.

We are only commanded to love; therefore, we must pray. Love is kept alive by communication. When we don't want to commune with the one loved, love is either going or gone. But why must we prove the necessity of prayer when we understand what it is? There is no love without desire. Where our treasure is, there is our heart.

But our earthly treasure is so attractive, because it is visible, appealing to our other senses, quick to call up the emotions. That is another reason for the necessity of prayer. Our real treasure is not visible, nor does it immediately rouse our affections. God is present, and after faith has established that fact, it must still supply the rest. Love is kindled mediately, by means of loving thought. By prayer God is vividly present to us, we get to know Him, and know Him as supremely lovable. Without prayer He remains a set of formulas in a dogma book. Prayer then makes Him real to us and He thus becomes our treasure. And prayer makes living and real for us the substance of faith and hope.

Of all prayer the noblest is liturgical prayer, for its principal agent is Christ praying as Head of His body. We shall consider here only the Divine Office. Of it Dom Cabrol wrote, "This official prayer is unquestionably better than any other, because it is the prayer of the Church inspired by the Holy Ghost, and brings the Christian into communion with the universal Church."[5]

The Divine Office, we must note, is, first of all, Christ praying. The liturgy in general is the priestly activity of Christ in the Church. "The Church, then, faithful to the mandate of her Founder, continues the priestly office of Jesus Christ, and does this primarily through the Sacred Liturgy."[6] In the Office He adores the Father, gives Him praise, thanksgiving, and reparation, and asks for what His members need to come to the beatific vision. He prays for the other sheep that they too may come into His unity. He does this through

---

[5] Fernand Cabrol, O.S.B., *Liturgical Prayer* (Westminster: The Newman Press, 1950), p. 151.

[6] Pius XII, *Mediator Dei* (New York: Paulist Press), no. 3.

us, through our intellects, wills, voices, emotions, all in us that are combined in praying the Office. So while He prays to the Father through our prayer, we are actually praying through Him, our Mediator, in whom alone our feeble communication has value. The staple of the Office is the Psalms, those prayers inspired by the Holy Spirit in the form of Hebrew poetry. That Christ knew the psalms, probably by heart, is evidenced by His spontaneous use of them. Christ quoted the following: Psalms 6, 8, 21, 30, 34, 68, 109, and 117. Three of the seven last words were quotations from the Psalms. And the words which St. Paul puts into the human intellect of Christ at the instant of the Incarnation are from Psalm 39.[7] We must realize that when we are praying the Psalms we are continuing this same form of prayer which must surely have been a substantial part of Christ's loving communication with the Father. He is still doing this through us.

The Divine Office is the official prayer of the Church. This is a second reason for its dignity. But it is also a reason for its objectiveness. It is not in itself the personal prayer of the one praying. Rather it is the prayer of one who is vitally interested in the interests of the Church. The Office will make us get out of ourselves and into the lives of the other members of the whole Christ. We shall be concerned for the Church in countries hostile to it. And our reading about persecution in these places will send us back to our Office with an attention and interest we never had before. We are now conscious that these modern

[7] Hebr. 10:5–7.

martyrs are praying through us. When we take the universal Church to Office with us we begin to realize that we are officially praying as members of the Mystical Body.

What need we say of attention at Office? We have much motivation to be attentive as well as method, arising from the nature of the Office and its dignity. Since Christ is praying to the Father in and through us, attention is first of all a remembrance of this. And on the feasts and during the more solemn seasons of His cycle, the temporal, the Psalms assume a different shade of meaning, depending on whether it is the suffering Christ, the glorious Christ, or the working Christ praying. On the feasts of our Mother and the saints, He is praising the Father for them and for what He recognizes of Himself in them. Since the whole Mystical Body prays in and through us in the Divine Office, we must remember this from time to time. Of course we cannot exclude ourselves, our needs, and our moods. We are members of the whole Christ too, and we may make this official prayer very personal; it must express us. But we are first expressing Christ and the Church, for that is the nature of the Office and of our obligation.

We may come to undervalue our community prayers because they don't change and hence tend to become monotonous. Let us realize their purpose and their nature. These particular prayers were either composed or selected by the Founder because they expressed the spirit of the community and would help maintain that spirit. Too, he deemed that they, at the times which he determined, would aid our communication of love, especially in a busy day. And being community prayers they would be the community's corporate expression of its desire for God with the resulting acts of adoration, praise, thanks, reparation, and petition. We must learn to relate these prayers to the liturgical year, which is the proper setting of our spiritual life.

We extract from the Foreword of the *Manual* of the Society of the Divine Word a good summary of the reasons for community prayers: "Our Blessed Savior has promised that, 'Where there are two or three gathered together in My name, there am I in the midst of them' (Matt. 15:20). By these divine words a special blessing is attached to vocal prayers recited in common. May we in our Society the world over cherish uniformity in our mode of prayer and unanimity in our spirit of prayer. Thus shall we promote love for our Society and for each of its members, and thereby also foster faithfulness to our holy vocation and happiness therein."[8]

INDIVIDUAL PRACTICES

1. Meditate on Christ's prayer to the Father.
2. Examine the nature of your own prayer.
3. Make your prayer today truly a communication of love, the expression of desire for God.
4. Examine past friendships that died because of lack of communication.
5. Where is your treasure?
6. Realize during Office that it is Christ praying, glorifying the Father.

---

[8] *Vademecum S.V.D.* (Techny: Mission Press, 1948), p. 5.

7. Take the Mystical Body with you to Office.
8. Collect favorite passages from the Psalms for recollection.

GROUP QUESTIONS AND ACTIVITIES

1. Discuss Christ's prayer for unity, John 17, in the light of what was written of prayer in this chapter.
2. Defend the fact that the substance of prayer is God.
3. Discuss the difficulties in love of God.
4. What are the helps to love of God, not available in your love of others?
5. Hold a study day on the Psalms.
6. Prepare commentaries on certain psalms from their use in the "Propers" of the temporal cycle.
7. Prepare appropriate psalms for choral reading, especially those of Messianic character. These could be done in a contemporary setting.
8. Conduct a study of the community prayers as expressing the spirit of the community.

CHAPTER 17

Mental Prayer

> **What I hope to achieve:** *To realize that mental prayer admits of stages.*
>
> **To synthesize the previous chapters:** *My glory to the Father now and in the beatific vision consists in my being for Him another Christ. This will be accomplished by uniting my will with His, through, in, and with Christ, by the power of infused charity. My love of God will express itself through prayer.*

In this chapter we take up spontaneous or mental prayer. Much has been written on this subject, and sometimes the reader has come away confused. Most practical advice has been given by the late Abbot Chapman, some of which we present here as a sort of theme for this chapter:

"Pray as you can, and do not try to pray as you can't."

"The only way to pray is to pray; and the way to pray well is to pray much."

"As to method, do what you can do, and what suits you."[1]

---

[1] *The Spiritual Letters of Dom John Chapman*, ed. by Roger Huddleston, O.S.B. (New York: Sheed and Ward, 1946), pp. 109, 53, 52.

We have already been instructed in this manner of prayer and have had some experience in it. Now is the time to look into it more deeply, to correct our mistakes, and to determine to use it well.

Mental prayer is spontaneous prayer resulting from thought. The thought may be our own, or it may be knowledge of God directly given by Him to the intellect. The latter, infused contemplation, will be considered in the chapter on wisdom, for it is an effect of this gift of the Holy Spirit. The thing to note about mental prayer is that it is essentially *prayer*, not thinking. Too often one gets the impression that it consists of some reading, a great amount of thinking, and a little praying. This is a fine method for spiritual reading; in fact, it was the method of the *lectio divina* of the religious orders in the Middle Ages. But it is hardly mental prayer. The latter usually begins with reading; reading gives way to thought, which, in turn, is transformed into prayer. We think only in order to pray, not to study, or resolve, but to pray. A resolution may, often should, be incorporated into our prayer, but it is not the end of mental prayer. When we have prayed well we automatically determine to be better. Such determination must follow. And mental prayer aims at praying well.

Within the past fifty years there has been "a great return to the ideas of antiquity and of the Middle Ages concerning contemplation and its place in the spiritual life. During the eighteenth and nineteenth centuries the idea had come to be accepted as well established, that, apart from special and unusual calls, the normal mental prayer for all was systematic discursive meditation according to fixed method: this was taken to be the lifelong exercise of mental prayer for those embarked on a spiritual life — priests, religious, nuns, devout lay-folk. Contemplation was looked on as something extraordinary. . . . Such was the common view, such the common practice, almost taken for granted at the end of the nineteenth century."[2] Thanks to the great revival of interest in dogma in our times and in the application of dogma to the spiritual life, the teachings of the Fathers and Doctors of the Church regarding contemplation have been revived, and it is seen once again as the normal development of sanctifying grace, charity, and the gift of wisdom. Prayer has been emancipated from the hold of meditation, and we are again free to pray as the Holy Spirit breathes.

We must go forward as He wills; hence, we must pray as He wills. It is presumption to say that anything else but meditation is esoteric, or not for us. The Church, in declaring St. John of the Cross a Doctor, has approved the soundness of his teaching in these matters. There are stages in prayer, and if God wills, we must advance in them.

The first stage is meditation. It generally follows a detailed method, e.g., that of St. Ignatius, St. Alphonsus, or the seminary of St. Sulpice, but the basic pattern of meditation is: reading, thinking, praying. As we have said above, in this stage thinking will probably predominate. On "dry" days one reads more, and one's prayer is made up of acts expressing one's weakness

---

[2] Dom Cuthbert Butler, O.S.B., *Western Mysticism* (London: E. P. Dutton & Co., Inc., 1951), pp. ix–x.

and lowliness, asking for help, grace to love God in spite of feelings, etc. Prayer may come at any time, during the reading and thinking, and there are times when it will predominate, but on the whole thinking characterizes meditation, as the very term implies. This is the prayer of beginners, who need some thinking to understand Christ, the principles and practices of the spiritual life, themselves and their difficulties, action and reaction.

But one will not stay with this prayer. As we advance in the spiritual life we find that a thought is enough to make us pray. The reason is that we have already done a good deal of thinking and much is understood, at least in general. Because of our deeper understanding we are more readily moved to pray. Should we stop this spontaneous outburst and return to thinking, because we are supposed to *think* in meditation? NO! Thinking has done its work, it has led us to prayer; hence we should now abandon ourselves to prayer. At this stage our mental prayer is a little reading, a little thinking, and much praying. Prayer may dry up, and, if so, we can always return to our book and our thoughts until it comes again. This stage is generally called affective prayer, because the prayer proceeds spontaneously from love.

God is simple, and advance in the spiritual life is advance in simplicity. So too our prayer becomes more simple. A mere concept, idea, or word can seize us so completely, can mean so much to us, that it leads us at once to prayer. And that prayer is also very simple, a word, phrase, or short sentence. Such was the prayer

of St. Francis of Assisi, "My God and my all." This
is a prayer of deep realization.

We may suddenly receive insight into the mystery
of the Trinity, or the Incarnation. The spiritual life
of the risen Christ, for example, may have a new meaning for us. Or the gift of understanding may pierce
us with the impact of a word of Holy Scripture. Our
thought and will are held, and our heart utters a
simple prayer, which it repeats over and over again.
This is a feature of this degree, which is called, ap-
propriately, the prayer of simplicity. Like those in love
who never tire of saying "I love you" or of repeating
the beloved's name, we spend the whole time of prayer
repeating a word, phrase, or sentence, slowly, perhaps,
tasting its meaning, seeking more therein. This form
of mental prayer is especially suitable to religious whose
spiritual life is centered upon liturgical worship, which
is full of texts that are themselves external graces. The
life of St. Gertrude is a good example of this.

There are times when even a simple repeated word
seems superfluous, and all we want to do is remain
in silence in the presence of God. His presence may
be vividly felt, or even slightly, but our desire for Him
no longer needs words; in fact, words are now a hindrance, for our intellect and will repose in Him without
the help of symbols. This stage is called the acquired
prayer of quiet and was much advocated by St. Teresa
of Avila. It is not infused contemplation, although it
is a special grace and often leads into that contemplation. We can acquire it by our fidelity to the leading
of the Holy Spirit in our love of God and in prayer.

While there is usually a progression from one degree of mental prayer to the next, it is also just as usual that one does not always employ the prayer of the same degree every day. One morning, for example, a person who habitually prays affectively may have to fall back on meditation. There may come whole periods when we can only pray according to the form of a preceding degree. The rule, remember, is this: Pray as you can; don't try to pray as you can't. One degree may be more advanced than another. But for us the "most advanced" degree is that which the Holy Spirit gives us *now*.

The next degrees of prayer belong to infused contemplation. We cannot merit them; we can only prepare and pray for them. Since they are the normal development of our supernatural life, God may give them to us. The important things to know now are that there is a progression in prayer, that the four degrees outlined in this chapter are possible by our own efforts and grace, and that infused contemplation, entirely God's gift, supposes the essential union with Him through our will, generally well tried and stable.

Need we have method in our prayer? No, but we must have order, if for no other reason than that order is natural. A detailed method is most practical for beginners, and it helps on "dry" days. We have mentioned some that are well known and helpful. But a detailed method is chiefly for beginners, it must be considered only as a *means* to prayer, not an end, and it may be varied as one feels the need. St. Ignatius has been most wronged by those who insist that he intended his "method" to be used continually. St. Ignatius, in fact, gave several methods in the *Exercises*, but these others are not so generally known. He intended his followers to be completely at the disposal of the Holy Spirit in the matter of prayer, to use or dispense with method, to use his or arrange their own.[3]

A basic order for prayer would embody these elements:

1. A preparatory prayer which would result in the needed dispositions: realization of God's presence, adoration, contrition, complete dependence on Him for grace.

2. Reading.

3. Thinking. The Sulpician method makes one first consider the subject of meditation in Christ, rather than in self, and this agrees with the advice of St. Teresa: "As I see it, we shall never succeed in knowing ourselves unless we seek to know God: let us think of His greatness and then come back to our own baseness; by looking at His purity we shall see our foulness; by meditation upon His humility, we shall see how far we are from being humble."[4]

4. Praying. Prayer here should be spontaneous, arising from our thought. But if we have been meditating on Christ's mysteries or words, our prayer will surely include acts whereby we adore Him, praise Him, thank Him for this act or word, love Him, beg His pardon for our failures in this regard, give ourselves to Him

---

[3] Cf. Alexandre Brou, S.J., *The Ignatian Way to God* (Milwaukee: The Bruce Publishing Co., 1952), Chap. 2: "St. Ignatius and Prayer."

[4] Quoted by Père Marie-Eugene, O.C.D., *I Want to See God* (Chicago: Fides Publishers Association, 1953), p. 46.

that He might relive this mystery and all His mysteries in us and through us, beg Him for this grace, merited by the mystery.

5. Thanksgiving for the graces God has given us during our prayer, petition that it be fruitful, effective.

Of course the prayer of simplicity may go at once to the fourth step. We must remember: freedom to pray.

What should be the subject of our prayer? What else but the life of our Head, which we are bound to reproduce. If Jesus is to live in and through us, if we are to take His place, we must know His earthly life. We may depart from this norm from time to time, having for subject our Blessed Mother, the saints, the principles of the spiritual life, our particular problems, but the Person of Christ should be the staple of our prayer. Let us always consider in each of His mysteries:

1. The exterior of the mystery: the action or the words themselves, the circumstances.

2. The interior of the mystery: Christ's intentions, His thoughts, virtues displayed here, His emotions.

3. The permanent effect of the mystery on the Church, and on us.

4. The saints associated with the mystery.

What a fruitful source for abundant and spontaneous Christocentric prayer is the life of Christ when considered in this way, and prayer that will develop into a like life.

INDIVIDUAL PRACTICES

1. Examine yourself on your habitual mental prayer.

2. Work out a basic method for yourself.
3. The test of prayer is its after effects, its results. After mental prayer are you more obedient and charitable?
4. Accustom yourself to employ prayer of adoration and praise more.
5. Relate mental prayer to the liturgical day.
6. Keep a notebook of thoughts on Christ's interior life.
7. Meditate on Christ's prayer of praise.

GROUP QUESTIONS AND ACTIVITIES

1. Discuss: "Pray as you can, and do not try to pray as you can't."
2. Isn't it safer to stick to meditation?
3. What are good methods of staying awake? What is the best time for mental prayer?
4. Conduct a symposium on the better-known methods of meditation.
5. Review and criticize various books of meditations.
6. Write out a meditation using the four aspects of Christ's mysteries.
7. Let each one make a study of the prayer life of a certain saint.

CHAPTER 18

Recollection and Reading

What I hope to achieve: *To realize the relation of recollection and spiritual reading to my love of God.*

Prayer is love of God communicating with Him basically by means of our desire for Him. Therefore, prayer is a continual thing. We don't go to prayer and come away from it; it is not an exercise, it is a constant in our life. It assumes different forms and is more intense at different times, but it runs through our day as a basic desire for God. In the words of Joseph Mary Plunkett, it sees "His Blood upon the rose," looks for Him in every circumstance, scans everyone for traces of His face.

This habit of praying outside the set times of prayer has been called recollection, and it is the proper atmosphere of the loving soul. Although the early writers of the Church did not know it by this name, they knew the fact: "We ought so to do all things as if in Him dwelling within us . . . ," wrote St. Ignatius of Antioch.[1]

We don't need to be convinced of the reasons for recollection. All that was said of prayer and its nature in

[1] *Epistle to the Ephesians*, Ch. 2, MG 5, 657A.

Chapter 16 certainly applies here. If we love, we pray, and as much as we can, for our desire follows our treasure, and is a continual employment.

But an added motive should be given here, drawn from the words of an anonymous Carthusian in the late twelfth century: "For when a godly soul enroundeth itself on all sides with the purity of internal meditation, no temptation, however violent soever it be, hath power to bring it into subjection by gaining its consent thereto, if as soon as temptation beginneth knocking at the door of the heart, it were wholly occupied with pure meditation."[2] The recollected person is armed in time of temptation; the unrecollected is caught without his weapons. While he is hurrying to get them the enemy can gain an advantage. When love is kept alive and burning by means of recollection, it is infinitely more possible for us to overcome temptation out of love.

Furthermore, recollection prepares us for our set times of prayer, "As we wish to be during prayer, so should we be before prayer."[3] Without recollection the transition from work or recreation is too great for prayer to be possible immediately.

The busier we are, the more distracting and absorbing our work, the more we need recollection. In fact, we can say that recollection is the special prayer of the very active. Imagine those plunged in the apostolate with and without recollection.

Are we to have a method for this type of prayer? Practically, yes. Since recollection is not a set com-

---

[2] *Eden's Fourfold River* (New York: Benziger Brothers, 1927), p. 21.

[3] Cassian, *Collationes*, ML 49, 842A.

munity exercise and is really up to us, and since it is performed amid distractions, many of which are appealing in themselves, experience teaches that some form and order should be adopted. What should it be?

The answer depends on the individual, on his personal attractions. We shall list here a few methods that have proved effective:

1. Ejaculations, either indulgenced, taken from Holy Scripture or the Liturgy, or "made up." These ejaculations may be mental or vocal, but, to gain indulgences, indulgenced ejaculations must be vocal.

2. Realizing that in all actions and circumstances we take the place of Christ our Head, with His attitudes, words, acts, omissions, for His two intentions: glory to the Father and redemption of man.

3. Seeing God's will, therefore God Himself, in everything in our day except sin and fault — the practice of abandonment.

4. Realizing God's presence within us and in those with whom we come in contact.

5. Thinking over some text of Holy Scripture or the Liturgy that has particularly struck us. This is good for those whose occupation is not too absorbing. This was the way of our Blessed Mother, who observed Christ growing and living before her eyes, both in His hidden and public life, and "kept all these things carefully in her heart."[4] In the course of the liturgical year and in our reading of the Gospels we too observe Christ. As a Desert Father said, "The monk ought to be like the cherubim and seraphim, all eyes."[5] In our recol-

---

[4] Lk. 2:51.
[5] *Apophthegmata Patrum*, MG 65, 141D.

lection, when this is possible, we keep and ponder over
what we have seen.

Recollection must be our spiritual atmosphere, to
which we should return whenever we are free to do so.
Of course, for the sake of recreation we may have
thoughts that are not directly of God; good balance
for mental hygiene demands that we relax our mind
by different images and ideas. But the point to be made
here is that we should turn to the thought of God
naturally, easily, and, in time, preferably, that we come
to see all things in Him and Him in all. *Integrate* is
the word.

When a married couple, let us say, spend an evening
together, the husband may be reading and the wife
sewing; each is intent on his occupation, yet each is at
least subconsciously aware of the other's presence. If
the husband speaks suddenly after a long silence, his
wife doesn't look up surprised that he is there. She
knew he was all the time. This is what habitual recollection will do for us. Eventually, even though our
work is absorbing, we come to realize that God is there
all the time.

All religious rules enjoin silence, and there are two
reasons for this: to avoid sins of the tongue and to
facilitate recollection. A religious house in which silence
is not observed is not a recollected house, and one can
question its religious spirit. Silence is not an end, it is
not even a virtue, but a means. Love gives meaning to
it, and love of neighbor takes precedence. Therefore,
one can, and should, break silence for the sake of charity, but there is great danger here of rationalizing. To

tell another a little community gossip "to cheer him up" is hardly a good reason. To listen to someone who is truly in need and to try to help certainly is. We are so used to noise today, the "background noise" of radio, "piped-in" music and record players, that silence at first is unbearable. But love desires silence, prayer runs to it, and in prayer we come to realize that silence is the atmosphere of the Trinity.

Reading is vitally related to our love of God for it is also a means. Action follows being, and being for us humans depends on our habitual ideas. A being whose dominating force is charity depends on his ideas of God being clear, motivating, and constant. Such ideas of God come through prayer which is the result of the Holy Spirit's action, but reading is a great help. We can imagine the quality of the lectures or the state of the enthusiasm of a teacher who never feeds either by means of fresh ideas gained from professional reading. We have seen that spontaneous prayer usually begins with reading: the ideas we obtain develop into communication with God. Something similar happens with spiritual reading: the ideas we obtain from it strengthen our fundamental communication with God that is the union of wills. It is like letters from someone we love, which are at the same time a communication of love, and the source of images and ideas that keep love alive.

We shall need spiritual reading especially in the active apostolate when our work will be either attractive in itself, difficult, or monotonous. In each case we shall need help to keep our heart pure, our love of God first, to see His will, to love Him therein and thereby. Then spiritual reading will be help and strength and we shall look forward to it as a means of reinforcement. A religious who so regards it can never be dissipated.

We are surrounded by the media of a paganism, which, after the first step of divorcing man from God, has followed with the logical second step of doubting His existence. Much of what we have read and shall have to read, most of the television programs, not only ignore God but make the very existence of God seem hardly important enough to think about, what with all of these other fascinating considerations. God has been reduced to an obsession whose existence a skillful analyst can remove. Professional education demands that we be at least conversant with such a literature, and the latter has an insidious appeal and influence. Some of its ideas are certain to stick, some may linger into attitudes. We must not only remove these but also counteract them with Christian ideas and attitudes, to supply truth for those who are "ever learning yet never attaining knowledge of the truth. . . . For from thy infancy thou hast known the Sacred Writings, which are able to instruct thee unto salvation by the faith which is in Christ Jesus."[6]

We should read what is helpful; that is a good rule. Perhaps we have found a helpful book boring and turned to something more attractive or recent. A little examination on the current needs of our soul should convince us that a book which can change us for the better is too dynamic to be boring. On the whole we

---

[6] 2 Tim. 3:7, 15 (Conf. ed.).

ought to cultivate a certain good taste in spiritual reading, to prefer Holy Scripture and its commentaries, the standard lives of Christ, explanations and applications of dogma, and the spiritual classics. And of course we shall always find in the works of members of the community a source of our community spirit.

Masters of the spiritual life such as Abbot Marmion have seen in the words of St. Peter to Christ, "Behold, we have left all and followed thee"[7] the whole program of Christian spirituality: attachment to Christ, detachment from everyone and everything else.[8] In these first eighteen chapters we have studied the attachment process, in the next two we shall consider detachment. The logic of this procedure lies in the fact that if we are attached to Christ, we are *ipso facto* detached from whatever is not Christ. If a man is clinging to one object he can't possibly cling to any other. But we have noted that in this very attachment we have met opposition, and it is this opposition and how to cope with it that we shall next take up.

INDIVIDUAL PRACTICES

1. Examine self as to recollection:
   a) Are you habitually recollected?
   b) What kind of recollection do you employ?
   c) What are the difficulties?
2. For one day be very careful to realize in all activities that you are taking Christ's place.
3. If you broke silence today, what did you talk about?

---

[7] Mt. 19:27 (Conf. ed.).
[8] Cf. *Christ the Ideal of the Monk*, its general plan.

4. Experiment with different kinds of recollection until you find one that is appealing and helpful.
5. Make notes of your spiritual reading.
6. Make a list of the twelve religious books you've found most helpful.
7. Read some of the New Testament every day.

GROUP QUESTIONS AND ACTIVITIES

1. How is recollection possible for a teacher?
2. Discuss the suggested methods of recollection and their practicality.
3. Discuss: "A religious house in which silence is not observed is not a recollected house."
4. Discuss the relation between recollection and sanctity, recollection and defection.
5. Should a religious keep up with current literature, "best sellers"?
6. What would be a basic library for a religious?
7. Discuss spiritual reading that you have found helpful.
8. Discuss: "This book is too abstract."

CHAPTER 19

Self

What I hope to achieve: *To try to understand self, and my self in particular.*

Our end is to give God glory and our means is union with Christ in the Mystical Body and all that this union implies. Our happiness will be in proportion to our fulfilling our role in the whole Christ. What is the problem then? It is self. There is a struggle between ego and Christ, and it lasts all our life. Ego wants to be ego, not Christ, and its method of warfare is sometimes brutal, sometimes imperceptibly subtle.

By self is meant human nature, and at the outset there are three fundamental truths concerning it which we must realize and act on:

1. Human nature is good.

2. Human nature has been weakened as a result of original sin.

3. Human nature has been redeemed, reclaimed, by Christ.

Human nature is good because God created it. "God saw that all he had made was very good."[1] He created

[1] Gen. 1:31.

161

man, soul and body, intending this union of soul and body to be endless. Death, the disunion of soul and body, was a punishment for original sin.[2] Modern psychology and psychosomatic medicine have reaffirmed the fundamental unity of soul and body in man. It is time to stop thinking of the body as "the prison of the soul." In the union of the two consists human nature: body and soul are the necessary component elements of man. And in this admirable synthesis God united mineral, vegetable, and animal life with the spiritual. What God in His wisdom has united no one can possibly sever. To do so is to call the body evil. The Manichean heresy is the most dangerous heresy in the history of the Church, and it is always cropping up in the most noble disguises. The fact that it is thoroughly un-Christian has been forever proved by the fact of the Incarnation. "Formerly spiritualization was the goal, now it is rather the moulding of the whole of human life. The meaning of Christ's Incarnation for the Christian life on earth is being understood in a new light."[3]

The body as God's creation is good, and its union with the soul is good because such a union is necessary for human nature. Because of its interaction and necessary relations with the soul and its influence upon it, the body must be valued and understood if we are to have a spiritual life that is according to God's will. We should have a fundamental functional knowledge of the systems of the body and of their relation to the soul and its life.

---

[2] Cf. Gen. 2:17; 3:19.

[3] Josef Goldbrunner, *Holiness Is Wholeness* (New York: Pantheon, 1955), p. 22.

The emotions comprise an important area of psychophysical reactions, and we must understand their nature, their place in our life, and their danger points. Father Bittle defines an emotion as ". . . an affective mental state of the animal organism, following the cognition of an object or situation, characterized by strong feeling, by an impulse to action, and by physiological changes in bodily function."[4]

The history of an emotion has three phases: First, we perceive an object or a situation as a good to be desired or an evil to be avoided; second, we either desire or abhor it; and third, we experience certain bodily reactions. According to the definition our desire or abhorrence is strong, vehement, at least to a degree necessary to produce bodily changes. Before we can have an emotion, therefore, our own reaction to the desired or dreaded object must be strong, and bodily changes must result.

Let us take sadness caused by homesickness as an example. We perceive our present situation to be an "evil," because it is not our home. We experience a repugnance for it and long passionately for the home we have left, which now becomes a most desirable good. We are sad, because we must accept this "evil" and relinquish the "good." One bodily reaction to this sadness is the refusal of the digestive glands to function normally, resulting in loss of appetite.

Scholastic philosophy divides the emotions into concupiscible and irascible. The former are primary emo-

---

[4] Celestine N. Bittle, O.F.M.Cap., *The Whole Man: Psychology* (Milwaukee: The Bruce Publishing Co., 1948), p. 257.

tions reacting to good or evil when the attainment of the desired object is possible without great difficulty. The latter are evoked by the presence of such an obstacle. The concupiscible emotions are: *love* of an object as good; *hatred* of an object as evil; *joy* in the possession of the good; *sadness* in the presence of the evil; *desire*, the tendency toward the good; *aversion* from a threatening evil. The irascible, also called the aggressive, emotions are: *hope* of obtaining an arduous good or of overcoming an obstacle to it; *fear* of losing a possessed good, or of a difficult evil; *despair* of possessing a good or of overcoming an evil; *courage* to make extreme effort to possess a good or overcome an evil; and *anger* because of a present evil. We can conclude that love is the basic emotion, for all the other emotions are caused either by a good which we desire or by an obstacle to our or others' good. While the prospect of joy in the secure possession of a good may be a motivating force, it is founded upon the initial recognition of and desire for the object as good.[5]

The emotions help us to fulfill ourselves as human beings. Each of us is a potentiality for perfection, each must be completed by the possession of the good which God wills for him. A house, furnished and ready for occupancy, is fulfilled only by persons living in it. Our tendency toward good and our abhorrence of evil are accomplished by the aid of the emotions. Although the

---

[5] Cf. Tanquerey, *The Spiritual Life*, no. 787; Geo. P. Klubertanz, S.J., *The Philosophy of Human Nature* (New York: Appleton-Century-Crofts, Inc., 1953), pp. 211–215.

intellect and will can, and sometimes do, choose good and reject evil without such aid, the usual human mode of this procedure includes the activity of the emotions. They fulfill a human need.

"In the ordinary course of events we should enjoy our spiritual life. Though God may withdraw His consolations from us from time to time, we were not meant to respond to God and the things of God in a continual spirit of stoic indifference. Our whole lives should be wrapped up in God — which means our whole personality. We *should* become emotionally involved, as well as intellectually and volitionally. Our emotions are every bit as much a part of our human nature as our soul and its faculties."[6] We must stir up our emotions in our reliving and continuing Christ's life. God meant them to be a help. We have no right to cause spiritual dryness. When it comes by way of God's will, that is another matter.

However, we must neither depend on the emotions nor live by them. If it is impossible to evoke them, we have to "hang on" by the will alone. Thus is our love of God tried and strengthened. We must learn to control our emotions, not letting them form the substance of our life nor get out of hand. They are a vital part of our human make-up as an aid to love, which is basically a spiritual process.

We should by now realize the important part played by thoughts and images in causing our emotions, and

[6] Joseph Lange, O.S.F.S., "An Approach to Religious Emotion," *Cross and Crown*, June, 1961, p. 175.

also in controlling or suppressing them. Thinking of an object as highly desirable, picturing it in colors provided by desire, are powerful stimuli to the emotions. And conversely, thinking of it in a different way, seeing it with a different perspective, can change or remove emotions. For example, we may be given a new work assignment which at first we consider to be an "evil." We react emotionally and are thoroughly unhappy. Then we decide to think of it differently. We replace the first set of thoughts and images with those which view the assignment as God's will, as an opportunity to re-live some phase or mystery of Christ's life; we think of the natural good points of the work and its circumstances. The new thoughts and images have produced new emotions which supersede the former, or at least have succeeded in suppressing the latter. It is imperative, therefore, if we are to live a healthy and supernaturally motivated emotional life, to learn to control and discipline our intellect and imagination. Without this control emotionality, unhappiness, and sin result. Thoughts and images feed desire and fear, and to rid ourselves of these emotions, when they are wrong, we must rid ourselves of what keeps them alive. And, on the other hand, while we can never be completely free of unwanted desires and fears, cultivating the right kind of thoughts and images will generally insure our having emotions that help us.

Integrity is that happy state of human nature in which God rules soul and soul rules body. When this occurs imagination and emotions are completely subservient to a strong intellect and will whose primary object is infinite truth and good. But this state, a gift to Adam and Eve, was lost to their descendents, and it is the work of a lifetime to try to regain it.

This brings us to our second fundamental truth: human nature has been weakened as a result of original sin. Our intellect has been clouded, and truth is elusive; our will is prone to take apparent rather than objective good. Integrity is reversed: imagination and emotions dominate intellect and will. The beautiful unity of soul and body planned by God, patterned according to the image of the unity of the Trinity, has split into a most harmful dichotomy, soul versus body. For the sake of the sensual the proper functions of the intellect and will are denied; for the misguided ascetic, the body is barely tolerated as a necessary evil.

In his primeval unity the human person directed himself, body and soul, to God as his end, integration in whom meant integrity for the parts of the person. But in our weakened state we know that a perverted integration takes place; man does seek some sort of unity, even if a degraded one: the body and its passions absorb the activities of the soul. The moderns have thereby concluded that there is no soul. And the resultant "unity" battles against God incessantly. The moderns have therefore explained away God, but their eternal explanations are only affirmations of their fear of Him, therefore of their belief. The soul still lives and breathes, although in prison. Added to this is a body open to every sickness and hurt, and fearful of death.

Our experience with confession has revealed what spiritual writers refer to as the predominant fault. One or several faults provide the staple of each confession, and we can't seem to make any headway. Our trouble is that we take the symptom for the cause. A headache is a symptom, i.e., a sign that there is something wrong within. There could be a number of things wrong: eye strain, hunger, nervous tension. Any of these three could cause the headache. If we take an aspirin we do not cure the cause, as a rule; we only remove the symptom. The aspirin will not fill the stomach or ease the eye strain. Hence the headache may recur. So it is with our predominant sin. Sin is a symptom, and if we only work on *it*, sin can recur. We have to remove the cause of which our sin is the symptom. St. John has reduced these causes to three: pride, sensuality, and possessiveness, the three concupiscences.[7] Concupiscence is disordered desire, therefore these causes can actually be reduced to one — the desire of an object other than God for its own sake. Right order demands that God be the first, and, if necessary, the sole object of desire. Some spiritual writers refer to the three concupiscences as well as the other emotions as ruling passions. We shall call them the basic weaknesses.

Pride is self-centeredness. Self is the center not only of our own life but also of the lives of all who have any lasting relations with us. In practice, self is the center of the whole of creation. Everyone and everything are viewed subjectively. Self is the sole object of desire, self is our ultimate end.

Sensuality is the disordered love of sense pleasure and

---

[7] 1 Jn. 2:16.

includes sloth, love of ease. The pleasures of sex desired for their own sake belong to sensuality.

Possessiveness wants to acquire: things, sights, news, money, persons. It sees something and has to have it, not for use, but for the satisfaction of being able to say, "This is mine." It is especially insidious in our relations with others, for often we don't recognize it for what it is. What we fancy is a desire to help others, even to bring them to Christ, may be nothing else than an inordinate desire to acquire them, to add them to our "court."

These basic weaknesses are the result of original sin; they comprise the enemies of integrity. In the state of original justice these weaknesses were not present. There was in man, however, a necessary interest in self, a healthy activity of the senses, and a desire to use what was needed for self-preservation. These operated under the strict control of intellect and will, which, in turn, were controlled by God. As a result of sin, these endowments of nature became inordinate. Man's integrity was lost. In our efforts to restore this integrity in ourselves we can make no true and effective progress unless we know our basic weakness (or weaknesses) and begin restoring it to order. This is very profitable matter for retreats and days of recollection. In fact, the work of restoring the three of them to the order of integrity is what we contract to do by our three vows: pride, by obedience; sensuality, by chastity; possessiveness, by poverty.

In the beginning of the chapter we stated that the great struggle in the spiritual life is between ego and

Christ: self does not want the life of the Mystical Body, which is Christ's life. Self wants to live its own life, but without integrity its own life becomes its own death. The three basic weaknesses sum up what self desires, and when these are analyzed we discover that self desires self. Its religion is the cult of self. We must at this point look deeply into ourselves to see what is our religion: Christ or ego? It can only be one or the other. Even a genuine humanitarianism is outer-fringe Christianity, for it seeks charity for Christ in need without knowing that it does.

There are two allies in the cult of self, the world and the devil. The world, in this sense, is creation considered apart from God, either as an end in itself, or not as a means to God. This definition would include the world both as a source of sin and a source of worldliness. We need not labor the point that creation is good, and we have already quoted St. Ignatius on its relation to our attaining our ultimate end. But we must face up to several realities: we must live to some extent in the world, we can never, even in the cloister, escape creation; the world can be attractive; the world is visible, God is not; and we do not possess integrity. The idea of the secular institute is that its members live in the world and sanctify themselves by means of the world. The term they employ for this is *secularity*. How do we sanctify ourselves by means of the world? By choice, by holding fast to God's will in every circumstance, choosing every person and thing primarily *because* He wants this, and, in what we have to accept, going *through* it to Him, whom we choose. "I do not pray you to take them out of the world, but only to preserve them from its evil influence. The world finds nothing kin in them; just as the world finds nothing kin in me."[8] Christ's way must be ours: the Father was His end, creation merely a means.

The devil is a great ally of self, but his role is not realized because so often he has been reduced to an anthropomorphic caricature in whom we can't quite believe. Satan has no form; he, or it, is a real person, with brilliant intellect — that of a fallen angel — and strong, one-tracked will, and is strictly a spirit. God's aim in permitting the limited activity of the devil and his cohorts is to try us, to strengthen us, to convince us of our own powerlessness and of His omnipotence. The devil's aim, however, is to win us from God and bring us into subjection to himself. He can act on our imagination, on our bodily appetites with their emotions, and can arouse sexual concupiscence. He cannot act on our intellect and will directly, since these are powers of the soul. God limits him, and will not allow us to be tempted beyond our strength.

If the influence of Communism is great, persuasive, and subtle, how much more that of hell, how much more persuasive and subtle its tactics? We must believe in hell and the devil and be on guard, as an F.B.I. man is on his guard against the infiltration of Communism. In time of temptation we must retreat, run at once, from the matter of the temptation to God by prayer that is confident of His power. We must have confidence in the sacraments and sacramentals, and contempt for the

---

[8] Jn. 17:15–16.

devil, for his aim and the foulness of his means, and for his final eternal defeat.

We are weakened, we are besieged within and without, but, we must always remember, human nature has been redeemed by Christ. While St. Paul is crying out in dismay because of the battle waging within him, he knows this: "Who will rescue me from this body doomed to death? Thanks be to God! Through Jesus Christ our Lord (rescue is effected)."[9] Since the Redemption we are no longer under the headship of Adam, the cause of our weakened condition. "Are you not aware that your bodies are members of Christ's body?"[10] "If, then, any man is in Christ, he is a new creation; the old state of things has gone; wonderful to tell, it has been made over, absolutely new!"[11]

And the renewal comes from the Holy Spirit, causing a new creation, through Christ. "When you send forth your spirit, they are created, and you renew the face of the earth."[12] By the grace of Christ we are what we are, and we remain and grow: members of the whole Christ, continuing His earthly life. We have the divine life, the infused virtues, the gifts and actual grace.

We have taken a look at nature in this chapter. We have seen it as self, opposing God as well as its own best interests. But we must also look at its good points: natural good qualities, talents, abilities. We must know our strong elements, for grace does not build on a weak foundation. And we should know our attractions in the spiritual life, to what we are more naturally drawn. The Holy Spirit acts through these too.

[9] Rom. 7:24–25.
[10] 1 Cor. 6:15.
[11] 2 Cor. 5:17.
[12] Ps. 103:30.

INDIVIDUAL PRACTICES

1. Examine yourself as to your attitude toward the emotions, and to their activity in your life. Which ones do you habitually experience?
2. What are your habitual desires and fears?
3. Examine yourself as to the role of the imagination in your life.
4. What is your basic weakness (or weaknesses)?
5. Attack this for a while by means of the particular examen.
6. Could you be called worldly? How can the world be for you a means of loving God?
7. What are your natural good points, talents, assets?
8. What are your attractions in the spiritual life?

GROUP QUESTIONS AND ACTIVITIES

1. Study the emotions in their three phases, using concrete cases.
2. Discuss: The emotions can be reduced to desire and fear, because they have love as their base.
3. Discuss the necessity of thought and image control for mental health.
4. Discuss: "Human nature as a result of original sin is depraved."
5. Discuss the relation of the three basic weaknesses to the different sins.
6. Read and discuss St. Ignatius' rules for the discernment of spirits. (Cf. Suggested Books.)
7. Discuss the influence of the devil in the religious life.
8. How does a religious become worldly?
9. Make a study of the four temperaments. (Cf. Suggested Books.)

CHAPTER 20

Mortification

What I hope to achieve: *To value mortification and to realize what mortification I need.*

To synthesize the previous chapters: *Glory to God and my happiness are achieved through Christ, through union with Him as my Head, continuing His earthly life. This means that my will is united to His in charity. My constant desire for Him expresses itself in prayer, and is strengthened by reading. However, the real enemy of my love of God is myself.*

By now we know that attachment to God implies detachment, not really from persons and things, but from self. Until we die, self will demand that it alone is the proper object of our love. But Christ has named the enemy and given us the principle for conquering him: "If anyone wants to be my follower, he must renounce himself, and shoulder his cross; then he may be a follower of mine. Why, he who would save his life shall lose it; but he who freely parts with his life for the sake of the gospel will save it in the end."[1]

---

[1] Mk. 8:34–35.

The principle is denial of self, but a problem immediately arises: how far should I go in this denial? Must I trim down my food and sleep to the barest minimum? Should I eliminate whatever gives me pleasure? Or should I work on the "eat what is set before you" principle, and consider my work, my religious exercises, the irritating and thwarting circumstances of my life, as self-denial enough? What about this "golden middle way"?

There is no problem: Christ is quite clear. We desire Christ, we unite ourselves to Him by means of the will, by love. Whenever and wherever the desire of self gets in the way of our love, self has to go; we must deny it its demands. Whatever self requires — food, sleep, recreation, friends, travel — we check to see if it is compatible with what we're actually and constantly doing — loving, willing Christ. That is, what we are interested in discovering is, does *Christ* want this? If He does, then so do we. We never ask first, do *I* want it? I am secondary. I have lost my life for His sake that *He* may live, that I might be the living gospel. My purpose, not as a religious but as a Christian, is not to live the story of my life, but the story of Christ's. This means a denial of what I want for *my self*. Always the question — is this *His* life? This is the extent of self-denial.

It is the principle of love of God, as we learned in the chapters on obedience and abandonment: we will what God wills because He wills it. Maybe it is some enjoyment, a form of recreation; God's will certainly intends such for us. We will it, not because self enjoys it, but *primarily* because God wills it. *Secondarily* we will it because it is naturally enjoyable. And we enjoy it. Just as it would be un-Christian to eat something delicious purely because it is delicious, so to eat the same thing primarily because it is God's will and deny ourselves the *enjoyment* of the taste would be un-natural. What we are forbidden is not the pleasure but the *pursuit* of the pleasure. Our pursuit is of Christ; the enjoyments are by-products.

Such a program of self-denial is as simple as it is categorical, but it is by no means easy. Are we able in every circumstance not only to ask, "What does Christ want?" but also, having got the answer, to do it? Is Christ always our primary concern? If we can answer yes, we need read no farther, we have arrived at detachment from self. But experience tells us that the spirit is willing, but the flesh weak.

We need exercise in self-denial so that when choice has to be made, especially when choice of Christ is difficult, we are not only able but also willing.

Exercise is provided by mortification, a term often used for self-denial. Here we shall regard it as a means to that basic denial of self, detachment, which results from attachment to Christ.

Mortification is twofold: that which comes to us from God, and that which is self-imposed. The former is far more efficacious because only God knows us perfectly, knows what we need to become another Christ and thus give Him the glory He wills, now and in the beatific vision. The duties of our state, therefore, are excellent mortifications at times, killing self-will and love of pleasures for themselves. Sufferings, mental and physical, are also very effective. Disappointments can teach us the emptiness of creation, of seeking creatures. Allied with disappointments are failures and tragedies. These really strip us of self. Then there are the "nights" of contemplative prayer (cf. Chapter 32) in which God takes us in hand and purifies us of the last traces of self-seeking before granting us the closest union with Him possible in this life. Yes, of the two kinds of mortification, that which God gives is better, because it is more effective. But while it is better and can certainly do the whole job of detaching us from self, it will not be effective without self-imposed mortifications. The reason for this is weakened human nature: if we don't voluntarily mortify self-seeking we won't willingly accept the mortifications God sends. We'll take, for example, the duty — we can't avoid it — but we won't take it as an effective mortification. But if we're in the habit of mortifying ourselves, we'll recognize the hand of God forming us into Christ in the mortifications that come to us from that hand. In practice, then, we need to practice mortification on our own initiative in order to maintain our weak will at the high level of seeking God first.

Let us look at some of the things we can do:

1. Mortification of the body: prompt rising, manual labor, avoiding comfortable postures and chairs, exercise and voluntary work in cold and hot weather, *etc.*

2. Mortification of the senses: abstention from smoking, soft drinks, useless travel (be honest), magazines and papers, TV, record players, movies, useless condiments and relishes, *etc.*

3. Mortification of the intellect and imagination: dismissing every unnecessary thought and image, practicing concentration,[2] dismissing any thought or image that would disturb peace, welcoming neglect, *etc.*

4. Mortification of the will: denying self every opportunity to exercise self-will, giving attention and interest to others, giving time, *etc.*

The etceteras have been italicized to suggest that the intellect, however weakened it may be, is still inventive. We must realize here that it is more important to mortify intellect, imagination, and will, without neglecting the body and its senses. Msgr. Escriva gives a warning in this regard: "Interior mortification — I don't believe in your interior mortification if I see that you despise mortification of the senses, that you don't practice it."[3]

The principle behind mortification is: God first, and kill everything in us that is sought primarily for itself. Therefore mortification is universal and it is continual, both from God as well as from self.

Mortification hurts, and we must face the fact. It does and it will. And another fact: we people today have been told, mainly by advertising, that nothing must ever hurt, that we must never suffer. Hence we have been conditioned from infancy against mortification. Not only by our fear of suffering, but also by our inordinate love of comfort, ease, fun, and speed. So we must be realistic, and realize three things: (1) we don't want mortifications because they hurt; (2) we don't

---

[2] Cf. Narciso Irala, S.J., *Achieving Peace of Heart* (New York: Joseph F. Wagner, Inc., 1955).

[3] Joseph Escriva, *The Way* (Chicago: Scepter, 1954), p. 54.

want mortifications because they make us give up comforts and sense pleasures; (3) but *we do need mortifications!* When we find something that hurts most to give up, there precisely is self making a last stand.

A wise practice for voluntary mortifications is that of the martyred missionary, Father Donovan, M.M. "Father Gerard Donovan, of Maryknoll-in-Manchuria, evolved a little plan of his own in these matters, a plan that became known to some of his intimates. It was to neutralize and sanctify his recreations and periods of ease by a special practice that included (1) a definite habit of offering thanks to God on every occasion of innocent pleasure that came his way, and (2) a cutting off of some little item in the program of rest or enjoyment, and returning it to God as a sacrifice of gratitude. . . . He had all the enjoyments that came to any other man, but he introduced a principle that made of them so many occasions to add strength along with the enjoyment. The principle was restraint."[4]

However, Venerable Francis Libermann, a strong advocate of voluntary mortification, prudently advises, "Small mortifications are a good thing . . . but I am not of the opinion that they should be continual, because they then become burdensome and are likely to make you impatient and troubled."[5]

It would seem prudent then to mortify ourselves as much as we can without losing our peace, without

[4] Bishop Walsh, *Maryknoll Spiritual Directory* (New York: Field Afar Press, 1947), p. 135.

[5] In Bernard Kelly, C.S.Sp., *The Spiritual Teaching of Ven. Francis Libermann* (Dublin: Clonmore and Reynolds, Ltd., 1955), p. 63.

becoming absorbed in mortifications. They are not an end in themselves. Love of God is our aim, our life; this must absorb us and prompt our self-denial.

Our mortifications must be suited, first of all, to our physical strength. When novices read the lives of the saints they are apt to want to imitate their austerities. Goldbrunner tells us that we must adapt these to the contemporary physique. "For constitutions like theirs [the saints] a strict asceticism was a wholesome antidote, for us it would be merely a useless attempt to deaden our appetites (would that we had appetites to deaden!), to weaken the pining flesh, and still further to exhaust a body which our voluptuously living forefathers have left us too exhausted already. What we need are spurs to force us into life, not a bridle to curb an exuberant *joie de vivre*."[6] While we may not agree with Goldbrunner as to the cause of our exhaustion, his conclusion is good: we need mortifications to "pep us up," "spiritual vitamin pills." And because of the softness of our times, the accent on sense gratification and comfort, our weakened, pampered physiques need the strength that comes from denial.

Our mortifications must also be suited to our moral strength; therefore, we should not do too much all at once. Here our spiritual director is needed lest we be imprudent. In fact, we should give our director at least a general plan of our voluntary mortifications, a practice to be kept up all our life. Remember the constant enemies of self-denial through which the devil operates: imprudence, pride, rationalizing.

---

[6] Goldbrunner, *Holiness Is Wholeness* (New York: Panthem, 1955), p. 20.

Finally, our mortifications must agree with the duties of our state. Care must be taken here to mortify without harming and to mortify without rationalizing.

In all of our mortifications we are taking up the cross, which is suffering according to God's will. Our life is the continuing of Christ's earthly life; how can it be easier, softer, more comfortable than His? Therefore, in the words of St. Ignatius: ". . . the better to imitate Christ our Lord, and to become actually more like to Him, I desire and choose rather poverty with Christ poor, than riches; contempt with Christ contemned, than honours; and I desire to be esteemed as useless and foolish for Christ's sake, Who was first held to be such, than to be accounted wise and prudent in this world."[7] The life of Christ is our norm. If in doubt as to practice a mortification or not, we should ask ourselves, "What does *Christ* want to do?"

INDIVIDUAL PRACTICES

1. Is there anything in your life that opposes your love of God?
2. Do you intend the enjoyable things in your life primarily because God wills them?
3. Do you accept as mortifications of self those that come to you from God?
4. Do you regard the mortifications deriving from the Rule and Constitutions as means of love of God?
5. What voluntary mortifications do you need?
6. Resolve to adopt Father Donovan's practice.

---

[7] St. Ignatius Loyola, *The Spiritual Exercises*, no. 167.

7. Ask your spiritual director's permission to practice the mortifications you have decided on. Ask him to recommend others.

GROUP QUESTIONS AND ACTIVITIES

1. What are the best mortifications for our times?
2. Discuss: You need mortifications more than did the people of the Middle Ages.
3. Discuss: Defection in the religious life could have been prevented by mortification.
4. Relate balance, moderation, and mortification.
5. Discuss: Your life provides you with enough mortifications.
6. Discuss: But you need more contemporary forms of recreation today. After all, didn't the late Pope tell religious to adapt?
7. Debate: Resolved, that television in religious communities should be abolished.
8. Discuss the relation between mortification and zeal.

CHAPTER 21

Prudence

> **What I hope to achieve:** *To understand and value the virtue of prudence.*
>
> **To synthesize the previous chapters:** *Glory to God and my happiness are achieved through, in, and with Christ. My love expresses itself in prayer and is strengthened by reading and mortification.*

We have studied in the first twenty chapters our end, the essence of union with God, our enemies to that union, and means of combating them. We shall in the remaining chapters study the other powerful supernatural means rewon for us by Christ's sacrifice and given us by the Holy Spirit.

The theological virtues have God as their direct object as well as motive. The moral virtues have Him at least as their indirect object, and always as their primary motive. The moral virtues exist on the natural plane as well as on the supernatural, with human objectives and motives, and we must practice these as well. To this end we shall preface each chapter on the moral virtues with a brief study of the natural virtues. A discussion of the natural virtues is necessary because of the relation between nature and supernature. Grace builds on nature.

The infused moral virtues are aids and supplements to the theological virtues.

"The exercise of the moral virtues pertains to the integrity of Christian perfection because these virtues remove impediments which would make the exercise of Charity itself either absolutely impossible or at least more difficult. Moreover, the moral virtues make possible the submission to Charity of all human acts not elicited by the theological virtues, and they allow of such acts being directed by Charity to the ultimate end." The moral virtues must be ". . . commanded by Charity or at least directed by it in some way to the ultimate end, since Charity is the only virtue which tends formally towards God, the Ultimate End."[1]

Some priests and religious are rightfully accused of immaturity by the laity. Those so accused have never grown up. To prevent this from happening to us we must know the marks of maturity:

1. The ability to face reality.

2. The ability to judge objectively.

3. The ability to accept responsibility and to be responsible.

4. The ability to realize ends.

5. The ability to realize the means.

6. The ability to use the best means to an end.

The last three marks characterize the natural virtue of prudence. We may also call it common sense. A

[1] De Guibert, *Theology of the Spiritual Life* (New York: Sheed and Ward, 1953), pp. 64–65.

person acts prudently when he knows where he is going and gets there as efficiently as he can. Prudence does not necessarily mean speed. A prudent man knows how to wait because he knows that at times it is prudent to wait. But whatever are the best means to achieve his end he will employ.

Supernatural prudence is the infused virtue whereby a person is able to choose the best means to attain his ultimate end, the beatific vision. It is light given to the intellect, and is, therefore, the great virtue of choice, most important for our realizing the purpose of our existence.

Prudence, first of all, keeps the end continually in sight, always seeing things with reference to the beatific vision. It seeks first "the kingdom of God and what he requires of you" and is not anxious about secondary matters: " 'What are we going to drink?' or 'What are we to wear?' " aware that "your heavenly Father knows that you need all these things."[2] It threads its way warily through the visible allurements of the world, heading surely for the beatific vision.

Prudence knows that the best means thereto is to sell all in order to buy this pearl of great price,[3] to "do with speed now that which will profit us for all eternity."[4] "Really, which of you, intending to build a tower, will not first sit down and calculate the cost, to see whether he has the wherewithal to finish it?" We have the means, which Christ categorically indicates in the same passage: "None of you can be my

---

[2] Mt. 6:31, 33.
[3] Cf. Mt. 13:46.   [4] St. Benedict, Holy Rule, p. 11.

disciple unless he first renounces all his possessions."[5] It is the task of prudence to keep us mindful of this complete renunciation of self and to choose the best methods of carrying it out.

Prudence chooses the best means for us individually to reach the beatific vision, since each one is an individual. What will help one may not help another. Prudence knows how to use the past, to turn mistakes into means.

Therefore, by this virtue we determine more certainly right from wrong, reasoning from rationalizing. We need it to discover what state of life is in God's plan, for this is a vital means for the individual to reach his end. And prudence will show us what Christ wants to do in and through us, how we can relive and continue the Incarnation. Prudence, therefore, keeps the image of the Son clearly in our mind.

Prudence directs the other three moral virtues. For example, it co-operates with temperance lest moderation be in reality mediocrity, and it keeps fortitude from going to excess.

In general we can say that the domain, the field of operation, of prudence is God's will. There is so much of self-will in the spiritual life, and in the priestly and religious life.

Father Colin, the founder of the Marists, wrote: "I fear nothing more than to follow my own will. Man spoils everything."[6] This virtue will help us to pick

---

[5] Lk. 14:28–33.
[6] Ven. John Claude Colin, S.M., *Principles of the Spiritual Life* (Harrow: Paschal Press, 1954), p. 129.

from the confusion and contradictions in our own mind the clear will of God. We shall still have to think, to weigh both sides, to check and countercheck, but in all this process prudence will be a guiding force.

This is the virtue of discretion, "the mother of virtue,"[7] which works hand in hand with temperance to maintain a healthy balance.

We can see how necessary prudence is for all those who direct others in any way, but especially for superiors and spiritual directors. It is so easy for managers of work in the religious life to lose sight of the ultimate end, concerned as they have to be with material things. But the guides of the spirit have the important task of directing by sure ways to that end the trusting persons committed to them. How these need the virtue of prudence! A spiritual director must approve, forbid, change, adapt. A superior must do the same and, moreover, have final jurisdiction in the delicate matter of permissions: to tell whether the subject's request is God's will or motivated by self-will.

In our dealings with others in the apostolate prudence takes the form of adaptation, as we see in Christ's public ministry. Our words, actions, and omissions have to be suited to what will best win *this* person to Christ. This is "being all things to all men"; yet prudence will also dictate how far we should go. Grace builds on nature, and our adaptation must take into consideration our personality, and age as well as our state.

On the day of profession the new religious is able to say to God, "I in the simplicity of my heart, have joy-

---

[7] St. Benedict, *op. cit.*, p. 100.

fully offered all these things."[8] Through the years there is great temptation to take them all back: responsibilities bring the love of independence, activities crowd out spiritual exercises, greater freedom (and middle age) leads to comfort-seeking, etc. The old self will cry to be reinstated, it will crop up under a multitude of innocent and beguiling disguises. It is the role of prudence to pierce the disguise and discover self. We shall find prudence to be supernatural common sense, which will say to us time after time in a flat, matter-of-fact tone: "Look, this isn't going to get you to the beatific vision. whereas this will." We shall learn to listen to prudence.

INDIVIDUAL PRACTICES

1. Examine yourself on the marks of maturity.
2. Do you have ordinary common sense?
3. Are you anxious about secondary matters?
4. Are you convinced that the prudent way to the beatific vision is to "sell" all that you possess?
5. Do you see God's will in your life as providence directing you to the beatific vision?
6. Do you sometimes rationalize?
7. To what degree do you have the virtue of prudence?

GROUP QUESTIONS AND ACTIVITIES

1. Discuss the possibility of immaturity in priests and religious. What are the causes? What the cure?
2. How do you rationalize in the religious life?
3. Cite evidences of prudence in the Rule and Constitutions.

---

[8] 1 Par. 29:17.

4. History must be viewed from the standpoint of the Incarnation. "Man spoils everything." How is this true in history?

5. Give evidences of Christ's prudence, natural and supernatural.

6. Write a character sketch of a mythical religious, who through the years took back everything he had given to God. Include how he got that way.

CHAPTER 22

Temperance

What I hope to achieve: *To understand and value temperance and its related virtues, chastity and humility.*
To synthesize the previous chapters: *My glory to God and happiness are achieved through, in, and with Christ. My love expresses itself in prayer, is strengthened by reading and mortification, and safeguarded by prudence.*

Natural temperance is putting our desires under the control of reason. It is maintaining the proper order in human life: intellect and will ruling desire and fear. In other words, temperance means integrity. Its field of operation is the three concupiscences. Temperance is necessary for a life that is physically and mentally healthy, and was a virtue much valued by the pagan Romans.

Our contemporaries, however, have not the same regard. We gratify sensuality in every way that we can afford. And if we can't afford it we buy on credit. Hence we overstep moderation in amassing possessions (which are not completely possessed because not paid for). Luxuries have become necessities. Pride drives us to acquire these as status symbols; luxury is the fertile ground for unchastity. And more and more we are turned inward to the cult of self. More than the Romans our generation needs natural temperance.

Supernatural temperance is the same virtue — St. Thomas says it is the infused moral virtue ". . . which conforms concupiscence to reason . . ."[1] — except for indirect object and motive. Where natural temperance moderates food and drink, for example, for reasons of health, the supernatural virtue does the same for the sake of the beatific vision. The direct object is moderation in food and drink, the indirect object is the ultimate end, and the motive is the same end. Temperance, both natural and supernatural, can and should exist in a person: God wills our health as well as our reaching the beatific vision.

Temperance aims at restoring us to the integrity enjoyed by Adam and Eve. The infused, supernatural virtue lifts the integrity of the natural virtue to the supernatural plane, directing intellect and will above mere man to God, allowing man's spirit to fulfill its seeking.

It realizes that the right order for the supernaturalized person is God first, man second, and it maintains God as the center; it tempers sense pleasure, moderates, mortifying here, allowing there, while keeping a *via media* dictated by prudence. It preserves the right order in the person's regard for his own worth before God in relation to others.

Chastity, which is an aspect of charity, is also related to temperance in that it rules out inordinate sex pleasures. For the married sex pleasures are out of order

---

[1] *Summa Theologica*, I, II, q. 61, a. 5.

when they are contrary to God's law and contrary to the marriage bond. Marital chastity demands a twofold fidelity, based on charity. The chastity of the unmarried is a complete absention from sex pleasures as well as from those actions which directly prepare for those pleasures, because this is in accord with right order. The ultimate purpose of sex is the child, to be reared in the security of the family; consequently, apart from this purpose and its setting sex has no other purpose or function. This is the order that temperance imposes.

Since the motive of Christian chastity is love of God, it must be regarded as an expression of love. Marital intercourse should be primarily a manifestation of unselfish love that seeks its concrete form in the child. When a priest, religious, or devout layman denies himself intercourse for love of God, this denial becomes a manifestation, an act, of love of God, which can beget spiritual children. "There are those who bar themselves from marrying for the sake of the kingdom of heaven."[2] "He who is unmarried is concerned about the interests of the Lord, how he may please the Lord. . . . The unmarried woman or the virgin is concerned with the Lord's interests, is intent on being holy in body and in mind."[3] Every temptation overcome is a positive act of the love of God, because our will is choosing God rather than the pleasure. Hence, chastity need not be a negative virtue, an absence, a frustration.

Therefore the vow of chastity is an act of love, giving to God a sacrificial life of love. It provides for a union

---

[2] Mt. 19:12.
[3] 1 Cor. 7:32, 34.

with God that takes the place of and surpasses a marital union in purity of heart. Critics of the life of consecrated chastity have called it unnatural and thwarted. "Virginal love . . . is not an impediment to the full realization of one's personality. It is not only no hindrance to the fullest attainment of one's final end, but it promotes that attainment as nothing else can. It not only does not hinder the realization of a perfect personality; it is, very positively, the completion, the sublimation, the perfection of human personality. The reason is this: perfect chastity makes it possible for man and woman to possess most fully and completely in this world the God who alone can be the fully satisfying object of man's essential faculties, which otherwise is possible only in the heavenly life."[4] It is perfect chastity, therefore, not sex, whereby man is fulfilled as a human being.

Perfect chastity is a supernatural thing, a fact which explains and safeguards it. It has to be lived on a supernatural level if it is to be maintained. When love of God goes, chastity goes; whatever keeps love alive does the same for chastity.

The child is the end of sex, the child is the result of chastity. If we truly love God our mutual love will beget spiritual children, and chastity will insure that they be not only our children but also, and chiefly, His. Our love will cause us to love others and give ourselves to them to the forgetfulness of self. ". . . the apostolate will help considerably in seeing beyond merely personal

4 Dominic J. Unger, O.F.M.Cap., *The Mystery of Love for the Single* (Chicago: Franciscan Herald Press, 1958), p. 38.

problems. For consecrated virginity — let us repeat it again — is not an end, but a means. The end is to love God and men with all one's heart, with all one's being."[5] There is no danger in our love of others if we are attached to them but detached from self.

Humility puts a person in his place, before God and before his fellow men. It brings about right order in the opinion we have of our importance and spiritual worth. Thus it is related to temperance because it inclines us to moderate this opinion and seek the lowest place.

Humility is based on our realization (1) of the fact that God is God and we are His creatures, and (2) of our own weakness and sinfulness. From this knowledge come several more, and startling, realizations: all the good in us is from God, whereas from ourselves is our evil; in the eyes of God we may be, as to our spiritual worth, in last place. The truly humble man indeed believes that he is in last place. The result is a complete selflessness, which is humility in practice.

". . . when you are invited, go to the lowest place and recline, so that, when your host enters, he can say to you: 'My friend, come up higher.' "[6] God has given us grace and other helps, but we are forced to acknowledge that we have not made full use of them. If we had, we would be far advanced in holiness. Knowing God, knowing what we know, with all of our advantages, we have still sinned against Him. But some

---

[5] P. Hermand, O.P., in Chastity (London: Blackfriars Publications, 1955), p. 115.

[6] Lk. 14:10.

other person, perhaps a notorious sinner, may be higher in God's sight because he is co-operating with what God gives and permits to him better than we would, and without our advantages, who, if he were given them, might surpass us. We never know, so we safely take that last place. And one of the uncomfortable things about humility is that the more we remain in last place, the more certain we become that we belong there. The other uncomfortable thing: when we are humble we are certain that we aren't.

It is interesting to see how three great founders of religious orders, St. Benedict, St. Ignatius, and St. Francis of Assisi, treat humility. St. Benedict considers it as an over-all system of asceticism and develops it in twelve degrees. In summary his thought is as follows: We realize the excellence of God and our own nothingness, we know that we have obligations toward Him, and we fear His justice. Since the cause of our defection from Him is our desire, we choose the safe way of obeying Him in submitting our desire to a religious superior. In the course of our religious life difficulties only impress on us the fact of our sinfulness; what seem like injustices may be done to us, and we conclude that we deserve any ill treatment. Finally, we reach that stage of believing in our heart that we belong in last place. The more we take the relation between Creator and creature seriously, the less seriously do we take ourselves.[7]

St. Ignatius likewise bases humility on the fundamental realization that God must be obeyed; hence,

---

[7] St. Benedict, *Holy Rule*, Chap. 7.

his first two degrees make humility submission: in the first degree we choose God over riches and power rather than commit a mortal sin; in the second we do the same rather than commit a venial sin, and even prefer the loss of life. In the third degree humility is the desire to be like Christ, and here, even when there is no question of sin, humility prompts us to renounce riches, honors, and esteem in imitation of Christ.[8]

St. Francis, in keeping with the humility which made him call his Order the Friars Minor, clothe them in "mean garments," and send them out to beg, sees it as a genuine seeking of the last place, the conviction that "nothing belongs to us but our vices and sins," and a consequent shunning of vainglory and prestige.[9]

Thus it should be clear that humility is the foundation of the other virtues. Even faith, which is the acceptance of revealed truth on the authority of God, has to be based on an initial acceptance of God's position. On this twofold realization of ourselves in relation to Him and our neighbor the other virtues can be built.

At the Last Supper Christ washed His Apostles' feet and then addressed them: "Do you appreciate . . . what I have just done to you? You call me 'Rabbi,' and 'Master'; and you are right. That is what I am. Well, then if I have washed your feet — I, the Master and Rabbi — you, too, ought to wash one another's feet; for I have set you an example, so that what I have done to you, you, too, should do. Most certainly, a slave does not take precedence over his master, or an envoy over his sender! If you bear this lesson in mind, happy are you

---

[8] St. Ignatius, *Spiritual Exercises*, nos. 165–167.

[9] St. Francis, *Works*, p. 49.

in case you put it in practice."[10] Christ exhibits humility in practice — selflessness. He who had no reason to be humble submits His human will to that of the Father in the most perfect obedience, and bearing our sins becomes a servant in last place. We must through our selflessness continue the humility of Christ.

INDIVIDUAL PRACTICES

1. Make each invocation of Cardinal Merry del Val's "Litany of Humility" the subject for a particular examen.
2. Examine yourself on the practice of temperance.
3. What is the relation between your chastity and your love of God?
4. What are your weak spots in regard to chastity?
5. Meditate on your spiritual and other advantages and the little use you have made of them.
6. Imagine what you would be like if you were truly humble.
7. Meditate on the humility of our Blessed Mother.
8. Plan a completely selfless day.

GROUP QUESTIONS AND ACTIVITIES

1. Discuss: Contemporary living is injurious to health.
2. Debate: Resolved, that total abstention is better than moderation.
3. Make a study of temperance in the mind of the Founder.
4. Discuss chastity as a positive virtue in the light of Matthew 12:43–45.

---

[10] Jn. 13:12–17.

5. What are the best safeguards of chastity?
6. Write a character sketch of a humble religious.
7. What are the best means to be humble?
8. How does the Founder treat humility?
9. (For Sisters) Defend consecrated virginity against the fact that the whole make-up of a woman is geared to motherhood.
10. (For Sisters) Discuss: Pride is generally women's basic weakness.

CHAPTER 23

Justice

What I hope to achieve: *To understand and value justice and its related virtue, religion.*

To synthesize the previous chapters: *My glory to God and happiness are achieved through, in, and with Christ. My love expresses itself in prayer, is strengthened by reading and mortification, and safeguarded by prudence and temperance.*

Natural justice is fast disappearing in our culture. It is defined as that virtue which inclines us to give everyone what is due to him. Today, however, in a culture characterized by the cult of self, we are more inclined to deprive others of their due if self is going to suffer. And since justice, like humility, is a rock-bottom virtue, it looks as if the foundation of our culture is fast crumbling. Hence, even on the natural level, the matter of this chapter is most important today.

Justice is the virtue that is most allied with truth; in fact, it can be regarded as a form of truth. Truth is being as known; it thus depends on objective reality, demanding us to respect things for what they are; justice is the recognition of this objective reality in the domain of others' rights. A personal or a collective right *is*; it doesn't appear to be, nor is it *perhaps*; it definitely and objectively exists. Personal honor, which owes to every man the truth, is also justice.

Ways in which justice manifests itself, other than truthfulness and justice *per se*, are gratitude, courtesy, consideration, and respect. How many times we priests and religious fail here, expecting these forms of justice as our right, but never returning them. We sometimes overstretch the cloak of our state to hide the deficiencies of our person.

Justice in the scriptural sense — "But Joseph her husband, being a just man . . ."[1] — was the sum of all the virtues, a valid concept when we realize that if a person gave God, man, and himself their due, he would indeed possess all the virtues.

Supernatural justice, of course, operates with reference to the beatific vision and is motivated by it. Briefly, since what is true of the natural virtue is also true of the supernatural, only on the supernatural level, charity is of no avail without justice, just as abandonment is useless without obedience. Charity does not bind one to the extent of his serious inconvenience; justice does. We know this from the obligation of restitution. Objectivity is the key to understanding the importance of justice: there is, in the strict sense, no "obligation" of charity, for there is no objective right demanding our respect; but there is an obligation of justice, and one is not freed from it until he has paid the "last farthing." "Why do you not prefer to suffer wrong, to be de-

---

[1] Mt. 1:19 (Conf. ed.).

frauded? But you yourselves inflict wrong and fraud, and that on your brothers. Can it be that you are unaware that the unjust will not inherit the kingdom of God?"[2]

God's will is on the side of truth, therefore of justice; God always wills justice. Charity, the union of our will with God's, is willing what is and what has to be, because of Him who is Truth. Therefore, charity demands that in willing the good of God and of our neighbor we will what is due them. Love of neighbor will seek to give first what justice demands, whether in regard to property or person. It will give the refinements of justice: courtesy, respect, consideration, gratitude. And the motive is God, what He wills, and ultimately God in the beatific vision.

Obedience may be viewed as justice submitting to the authority God shares with His representatives.

The virtue that regulates our fundamental relationships with God is a form of justice — the virtue of religion. Inclining man to give God what is due Him, religion indicates the fourfold duty of adoration, worship, service, and love. Its object is every means whereby man can discharge this duty; thus, it is a virtue that directs our life, our every moment. "It is certain that all the Christian virtues are necessary for evangelical perfection: faith, hope, charity, and the moral virtues, among which the most important is the virtue of religion, which is justice in regard to God."[3]

---

[2] 1 Cor. 6:7–9.
[3] Garrigou-Lagrange, *Christian Perfection and Contemplation* (St. Louis: B. Herder Book Co., 1937), p. 135.

Religion is related to our primary duty of glory in that it is an infused power to give God the expressed glory of adoration, service, and love. Abbot Delatte has well expressed this bond: "Religion is a moral virtue, the most noble of all the moral virtues, and is akin to justice. . . . If we had leisure to write the history of any religious act whatever, we should note with theologians that it always implies an intellectual appreciation of divine excellence (formal glory), a humble self-abasement, the will to confess submission, and finally an actual recognition of the divine sovereignty, whether by way of an expressive act and confirmation of some sort, merely internal in character, or by an act which is at once internal and openly manifested (expressed glory). It is this last act which properly speaking makes the act of religion and worship, in which the glorification of God is consummated."[4]

Thus religion is concerned with more than worship as such: it embraces every duty we owe to God as the result of formal glory, the acts that prompt and lead up to worship, and worship's practical results of love and service. In brief, it is concerned with man's whole duty as creature and as rational being to God. "The virtue of religion is, after the theological virtues, our principal virtue; it effects in practice the inspirations of the theological virtues. Its exercise is the divine praise, but nothing in our life can escape its spirit, all that we do is for God's glory."[5] St. Thomas, in addition to

[4] Dom Paul Delatte, *Commentary on the Rule of St. Benedict* (Latrobe: Archabbey Press, 1950), p. 132. Parentheses ours.

[5] Père Gardeil, O.P., *The Holy Spirit in Christian Life* (St. Louis: B. Herder Book Co., 1954), p. 57.

recognizing a special value in acts which are produced directly by the virtue of religion and are its proper fruit, holds that all acts which are prescribed or determined by this take from this source a religious character. Actions of this last sort are innumerable in a religious life; because of the profound and total consecration of our very being to God's service there can scarcely be an act which escapes this transformation, provided we are careful often to renew and ratify our profession. " 'If a man devote his whole life to the service of God, his whole life will belong to religion.' "[6]

Therefore religious, who are bound to God by a total consecration, which is nothing else but a ratification of the obligations of baptism, have religion as their special virtue. Charity and religion unite them to God and give their lives their supernatural character.

In general, Christians today have special need for reaffirming the importance of this virtue. There is a decline of respect for authority. The position of the father is weakened; a premium is placed on youth, and old age is merely the subject for social security and geriatrics. We are not conditioned to admit our complete duty to our elders. The cult of self has caused a lack of respect, of healthy fear, and this is present in our attitude toward God. Emotionality in our spirituality, too, has resulted in a religion as unrealistic as it is shallow. It is time to return to fundamentals.

Religion is the root virtue of the human soul of Christ, and it must be ours.

[6] Delatte, *op. cit.*, pp. 134–135. The quotation is from *Summa Theologica*, II, II, q. 81, arts. 1 and 4.

"For this reason at his entrance into the world Christ says,

'Sacrifice and oblation you did not wish,
　but you have fitted together a body for me.
You took no pleasure in burnt offerings
　and sin offerings.
Then I say, Here I am; I have come
　to do your will, O God,
as it is written in the roll of the book.' "[7]

Our religion is nothing else than our continuing His religion, which is His realization of His duties to the Father as Son and as creature.

INDIVIDUAL PRACTICES

1. Mark passages in the Gospels indicating that religion was Christ's root virtue.
2. Meditate on the relation between religion and the vows.
3. Make necessary changes as to promptness, respect, consideration, gratitude.
4. Offer one Mass in the spirit of religion.
5. Offer the Office of one day in this spirit.
6. Be conscious of the religious character of one day.
7. Examine self as to whether you are the cause of others' "pet peeves."
8. Read the Books of Kings for spiritual reading.

GROUP QUESTIONS AND ACTIVITIES

1. Discuss the value of honor to a person, as a person and as a religious.

[7] Hebr. 10:5-7.

2. List your "pet peeves" in community life. (Charity with frankness here!)

3. Relate glory, charity, and religion.

4. How do tasks performed by religious such as bus driving, maintenance, have a religious character? Discuss all of the implications of religion involved.

5. Why are the Mass and Office religious acts *par excellence?* Defend the "time wasted" by choral recitation.

6. What are all the ordinary ways in which a religious could offend against justice?

7. Study the "man of God" and the "sons of the prophets" in the Old Testament from the standpoint of religion. Study justice as an important virtue in Old Testament spirituality.

8. Read aloud psalms that express justice and religion.

CHAPTER 24

Fortitude

What I hope to achieve: To understand and value fortitude, the special power of actual grace, and the role of Mary Mediatrix in my spiritual life.

To synthesize the previous chapters: My glory to God and happiness are achieved through, in, and with Christ. My love, joined to religion, expresses itself in prayer, is strengthened by reading and mortification, safeguarded by prudence and temperance, validated by justice.

The idea of natural fortitude is courage and bravery; it is not necessarily strength. A man may be strong and at the same time afraid to fight. A vulgar word perhaps best expresses it: "guts." Fortitude is the ability to withstand and face difficulties and to put up a good fight. The love of a fight need not be there, only the willingness to do one's best once it has begun.

Linked with this virtue are patience and perseverance. The former is the ability to suffer, to endure, or, to use another colloquial term, to "take it." Perseverance is "taking it" to the end.

Our contemporary living has not conditioned us for the practice of fortitude, patience, and perseverance. Comfort has led us to fold up under difficulties. Conformity tells us to submit rather than oppose, medicine and drugs have made it unthinkable to accept suffering willingly, and mobility has made stability unthinkable. We have much in our background to overcome; we must not be surprised at our lack here, but rather prepared. Fortunately there is supernatural fortitude.

This is the infused virtue which ". . . strengthens the soul in the pursuit of arduous moral good, without allowing it to be deterred by fear, even the fear of death."[1] This is our time of trial, we cannot expect perfect happiness. The sole qualification for the beatific vision is love, and now our love is being tested by difficulties. Since we are weak humans, the testing process is by means of "arduous moral good." Our way to the beatific vision is in Christ, with Him; the life of independent self has to yield to Christ's life, and here again is ground for difficulties: Self vs. Christ. We shall not attain the beatific vision until Christ is formed in us, on earth or in purgatory, but Christ will win out. "Yes, for the sake of Jesus every moment of our lives we are condemned to death, so that the living power of Jesus may become evident in our weak selves so liable to death."[2]

We can and must expect a continual battle, continual difficulties until we have surrendered self to Him. Fortitude is only possible when there is a goal, some-

---

[1] Tanquerey, *Spiritual Life*, no. 1076.
[2] 2 Cor. 4:11.

thing to fight for, and we Christians have two clear and glorious goals: proximate, to be made into Christ; ultimate, beatific glory. The end itself gives strength to one who has none of his own. But apart from our end, we have our greatest strength in the Mystical Body. "I can do all things in him who strengthens me."[3] We are joined to Christ in an organic union; we are weak of ourselves, but we are not alone. Our Head lives in us and through us. We are strong with the strength of Christ. "Gladly, therefore, will I boast of my infirmities, that the power of Christ may spread a sheltering cover over me. . . . For when I am weak, then I am strong."[4] That the difficulties in our life are God's will, or at least that they take place by His permission, should also give us strength. If He wants us to suffer difficulties, He will give us the power.

The Mystical Body unites us not only to Christ, and, therefore, with the whole Trinity, but also to the other members. Our merits may be few but their merits, as well as their prayers, are a source of strength for us. The praying Church is praying for us; we are not alone. The doctrine of the Communion of Saints must be a practical force in our life.

Supernatural fortitude strengthens the will, in the light of these other supernatural helps, for the life-long, day-to-day combat. Each era of history seems to have its own peculiar difficulties, and one that is the product of our own is conformity. That individualism should end in conformity is paradoxical, but true. We

---

[3] Phil. 4:13.
[4] 2 Cor. 12:9–10.

find it as a subtle foe of Christ and the beatific vision, and must deal with it, when necessary, with fortitude. "Those who pay attention to what people may say or do, will never accomplish anything. I act neither to win your affection nor your esteem. I am what I am before God. What men think of me will make me neither better nor worse,"[5] wrote Father Colin.

Fortitude is also the infused power to suffer with patience, whether the sufferings be mental or corporal. Most sufferings of religious are of the former kind, and many of these are either imaginary or exaggerated. As someone has wisely said, we don't have any large crosses, so we tend to make large ones out of small ones. Our real sufferings, however, we must welcome as an opportunity to relive Christ's life. Our Head has suffered, so must we. The way to the Resurrection is the Passion and Death. Our suffering with Him was a consolation to Him in His Passion, and is a means of reparation now, as well as a source of grace for others. What is wanting to Christ's sufferings is our co-operation in them. "By Thy holy cross Thou hast redeemed the world." Our apostolate will only have power through our taking up our cross, which is suffering according to God's will. Then, too, love is proved by suffering: where love is never tested one can never be sure. "For you have tested us, O God! You have tried us as silver is tried by fire."[6] "But in all those things we are more than victorious through him who has loved us."[7]

---

[5] Ven. John Claude Colin, S.M., *Principles of the Spiritual Life* (Harrow: Paschal Press, 1954), p. 118.

[6] Ps. 65:10.

[7] Rom. 8:37.

An integral part of fortitude is, of course, perseverance. "But he who holds out to the end will be saved."[8]
". . . so that never departing from His guidance but
persevering in His teaching in the monastery until
death, we may by patience share in the sufferings of
Christ, that we may deserve to be partakers of His
kingdom."[9] St. Benedict has in this passage given all
the elements of the theology of perseverance, and commentary is unnecessary. We would merely repeat his
idea that perseverance is "until death," and its aim is
that which should occur first, the death of self.

A form of perseverance is stability, a quality that is
difficult for us mobile, sanguine Americans. We enjoy,
and feel we need, change. We tire of our work and
hanker for something different, and thus is born an
"inspiration" and another permission. We need fortitude to "stay out," to hold on to patience, to let Christ
relive the monotony and the seeming uselessness of
Nazareth.

Fortitude is the virtue of martyrs, for it gives strength,
not only "until death," but also for death, if such be
demanded. "Death before sin" should become our attitude, conditioning us for the possibility of martyrdom.
We should be well acquainted with the sufferings of
the martyrs; these will be allies of fortitude in time
of great temptation.

The monastic life in its beginnings was conceived
of as a substitute for martyrdom, for the age of martyrs
was by then over in the Empire. It was in this spirit
that St. Benedict could quote St. Paul, "For thy sake

---

[8] Mt. 10:22.   [9] St. Benedict, op. cit., p. 11.

we are put to death all the day long. We are regarded as sheep for the slaughter."[10] The religious life is a martyrdom in that the daily death of self results in the affirmation of Christ. It is only when we desperately want self to live, that is, lack the spirit of martyrdom, that rules and orders become intolerable. They should be intolerable, then, for they have lost meaning.

Some fall into a kind of prudence that is really nothing else but fear. They hesitate to act even when they know they should; there is always one more deterring consideration. When pressed they invoke prudence and fancy that they are leading exponents of this virtue. In reality they lack it because they lack fortitude. Timidity was hardly one of the gifts of Pentecost.

Without going into a theological study of actual grace, its place and importance in our spiritual life should be considered here, because it is the ordinary strength of the soul, even of those in mortal sin. Fortitude comes to our aid for "arduous moral good" — and much in the course of the day can be arduous — whereas actual grace is needed for everything we do on the supernatural level. It is defined as a supernatural and transient help whereby God enlightens the intellect and strengthens the will so that they might perform supernatural acts.[11] We may say that actual grace is a sharing in God's power.

Actual grace can be inspirations, or "lights," given either intuitively or by God facilitating or guiding our ordinary thought processes. It moves the will with a

[10] *Ibid.*, pp. 30–31. Rom. 8:36 (Ps. 43:22).
[11] Cf. Tanquerey, *A Manual of Dogmatic Theology*, no. 898.

real power outside of us — God. What a strengthening thought it is to know that our weak wills are power-driven by infinite Power.

It propels us to the beatific vision by aiding us to turn everything into love. This is its specialty, to supernaturalize our lives. And we cannot do this without it. "Not that we are competent of ourselves, to take credit for anything as originating from us. Really our competence is from God."[12] Since we only come to the beatific vision in Christ, grace's constant activity proximately is turning us into Him.

Grace is God's action; therefore, our part is cooperation. Venerable Libermann was most insistent on our subordinate role. "He [Libermann] repeats unceasingly that the most perfect cooperation with grace consists in a total abandonment to the all powerful operation of God — the one thing He demands is that we be faithful to His grace, that we allow Him to act as He sees fit, without mingling our own action with His but 'await all motion and all life from Him alone.' 'We of ourselves cannot will anything in the order of grace. God supplies this willing. When we have it, we cannot of ourselves execute it. God gives us the means. Our role is to be faithful in following God's guidance, in allowing Him to do in us what seems good to Him.' "[13]

Our Blessed Mother is the mediatrix for us of all graces. Contemplating God in the beatific vision, she

---

[12] 2 Cor. 3:5.

[13] Bishop Jean Gay, C.S.Sp., *Spirit of Venerable Libermann* (New York: Society of St. Paul, 1954), p. 94.

sees her children and their needs and personally intercedes for all grace for all. Benedict XV wrote of this: "Because of the union of the Virgin to Jesus in His redeeming Passion, the graces of every kind which we receive from the treasury of the Redemption have been distributed to us, so to say, by the hands of the Virgin of Sorrows."[14]

By our Mother's intercession we have received from the blessed Passion every heavenly blessing and grace: sanctifying grace, the virtues, the gifts and daily actual graces. We are certain at all times of the interest and love of the Mother of the whole Christ.

INDIVIDUAL PRACTICES

1. Do today the most difficult things you are able prudently to do.
2. Adopt for a while, with your confessor's consent, some bodily austerity.
3. Read one of the "acts" of the early martyrs, e.g., of SS. Perpetua and Felicitas.
4. Relate overcoming serious temptation with martyrdom.
5. From time to time offer your sufferings with Christ's in the Mass.
6. Meditate on the force of actual grace in each daily activity.
7. Study and meditate on the proper Mass text for the feast of Mary Mediatrix.
8. Adopt the practice of meditating on Mary Mediatrix during the fifth glorious mystery.

---

[14] *Acta Apostolicae Sedis,* X, p. 182.

GROUP QUESTIONS AND ACTIVITIES

1. Discuss: Conformity characterizes our age.
2. Discuss: The religious life crushes individuality.
3. Hold a symposium on the "acts" of the early martyrs.
4. Study the Desert Fathers' way of life as a substitute for martyrdom.
5. Study the Communion of Saints.
6. When would fortitude be especially needed in the religious life?
7. What about the religious who habitually tells the superior, "I can't . . ."?
8. Consider in detail the day of a religious if there were no actual grace.

CHAPTER 25

The Gifts of the Holy Spirit

What I hope to achieve: *To understand the importance of the gifts for my life.*
To synthesize the previous chapters: *The unity of the life of the Trinity is the key to our own life as well as its pattern. We are made to the image of God; therefore, to the image of God's life. The divine nature is the object and occupation of the Persons of the Trinity; therefore it is to be our object and occupation. In the eternal will whereby the Father willed us to share in the occupation of God, there was unity, for the Father simply willed, as it were, one Person, the whole Christ.[1] Per Ipsum, Cum Ipso, In Ipso — Gloria! Our eternal occupation is one: the glory of love, based on beatific knowledge. Knowledge of Him is not our end, no more than is God's own knowledge of Himself: His knowledge is dynamic — the Holy Spirit is the love proceeding from that knowledge. Our occupation now is one: love. The other virtues are foundations, means, safeguards, or expressions of love. Christ is the way to the Trinity, the one way. For we cannot get to the*

---

[1] Cf. Émile Mersch, S.J., *The Theology of the Mystical Body* (St. Louis: B. Herder Book Co., 1951), p. 597.

Trinity except in the Person of the Son. Our eternal love must be joined to His and offered to the Father through His, as He loves through us His members. He is the glory of the Father. We will be acceptable to the Father only in our resemblance to His Son. Therefore our love now has one preoccupation: to reproduce and relive His life. For this supernatural transformation we need the mind of the Father telling us what we must do, what we must be. We are given this mind by the Holy Spirit, and for this purpose Christ merited for us the gifts. They enable us, to the extent and in the way that the Father wills, to be sons.

St. Thomas tell us that ". . . . the gifts are certain perfections of man by which he becomes amenable to the instigation of the Holy Ghost. . . . Therefore the gifts of the Holy Ghost are habits by which man is perfected to obey readily the Holy Ghost."[2] A modern exponent of St. Thomas adds: "The gifts are not to be confused with the inspirations of the Holy Spirit; they are powers in the soul making it receptive to the direct inspiration of the Holy Spirit, a sail to catch the wind of the Holy Spirit."[3] So we see that the gifts — infused in the soul together with sanctifying grace and the

[2] *Summa Theologica,* I, II, q. 68, a. 3.

[3] Père Gardeil, O.P., *The Holy Spirit in Christian Life* (St. Louis: B. Herder Book Co., 1954), p. 7.

virtues — are habits or powers enabling a person to receive the Holy Spirit's inspirations and impulses, given according to the nature of the gift. "The Holy Spirit, by inspirations corresponding to His gifts, presses us on to action, and in His hands we become no more than instruments. We lose the first place in the direction of our conduct; filled with divine assistance we have only to give our consent to His work; the task becomes easier; difficulties are eliminated."[4]

The work of the Holy Spirit is to form us into Christ, and to this end He must give us the mind of Christ, which is the mind of the Father in this regard. "The Holy Spirit . . . will teach you everything, and refresh your memory of everything I have told you."[5] This means that He teaches Christ in His totality. The gifts make it possible for us to receive this divine formation.

Father Lallement has indicated the "four kinds of lights to direct us in our actions. First, reason; which is very weak, and is not sufficient by itself to conduct us to our end. . . . Secondly, faith; which, by attaching us to supreme truth, supplies us with safe guidance secure from error. Thirdly, supernatural prudence; which being added to faith, makes us choose those supernatural means which are the most useful for attaining a supernatural end. Fourthly, the gifts of the Holy Spirit; which by principles more exalted, without reasoning, without perplexity, show us what is best, enabling us to discern it in the light of God with more or less

[4] *Ibid.*, pp. 6–7.
[5] Jn. 14:26.

of evidence, according to the degree in which we possess them."[6] We must note that the inspirations for which the gifts prepare us are not the product of our own reasoning processes. They may build on them, but they are always in their essence strictly inspirations, therefore they are given to us intuitively.

That the gifts are indeed necessary for our supernatural life has been well stated by De Guibert: ". . . no one can persevere in the spiritual life, as we have already pointed out, much less make progress therein, unless he be assisted by many impulses and inspirations of the Holy Ghost, to which he is more readily made docile precisely by the Gifts."[7]

The person who lives by the operation of the gifts is propelled by the Holy Spirit and acts with comparatively less effort. "There is a decided difference in the pursuit of the divine ultimate when it is regulated by human zeal and industry, or even by the infused virtues, and when it is formed according to the rule and measure of the Holy Ghost. For example, although the forward progress of a ship may be the same, there is a vast difference in its being moved by the laborious rowing of oarsmen and its being moved by sails filled with a strong breeze. We read in the Gospel of St. Mark that our Lord saw *his disciples straining at the oars.* They were making progress in the way of the Lord only at the expense of great labour, since each was proceeding by his own power and industry through his

---

[6] Louis Lallement, S.J., *Spiritual Doctrine* (Westminster, Md.: The Newman Bookshop, 1946), pp. 123–124.

[7] Joseph De Guibert, S.J., *Theology of the Spiritual Life* (New York: Sheed and Ward, 1953), p. 125.

own ordinary virtues. However, when the Spirit fills the soul interiorly, and measures it by His rule, then without labour and in a newfound freedom of the heart the soul moves rapidly like a sail filled with a breeze. The Psalms testify to this: *I have run the way of thy commandment when thou didst enlarge my heart;* and again: *Thy good spirit shall lead me into the right land.*"[8]

"It is the substitution of this regime of gifts for the regime of virtues, either acquired or infused (these last marking the transition), that constitutes the mystical state. The soul then becomes, more or less continuously, as St. Gregory Nazianzen says, 'an organ which the Holy Spirits blows and on which He plays.' "[9]

All of this may lead us to think that no activity is demanded on our part, but we must note well the fact that the gifts operate best in a pure heart. "The gifts do not subsist in the soul without charity, and in proportion as grace increases, they increase also. Hence it is that they are so very rare, and that they never attain a high degree of excellence without a fervent and perfect charity; venial sins and the slightest imperfections keeping them, as it were, bound down and preventing them from acting."[10] The free reign of the Holy Spirit occurs, St. Benedict teaches, only after the monk has climbed the twelve degrees of humility.

The gifts, it is clear, aid the infused virtues. We

---

[8] John of St. Thomas, *The Gifts of the Holy Ghost* (London: Sheed & Ward, 1951), pp. 56–57.

[9] Monk of the Eastern Church, *Orthodox Spirituality* (London: Society for Promoting Christian Knowledge, 1946), p. 74.

[10] Louis Lallement, S.J., *op. cit.*, p. 123.

give here a schema showing the relation of each to the other according to Father Garrigou-Lagrange:[11]

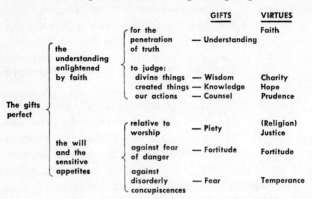

			GIFTS	VIRTUES
		for the penetration of truth	— Understanding	Faith
	the understanding enlightened by faith	to judge:		
		divine things	— Wisdom	Charity
		created things	— Knowledge	Hope
The gifts perfect		our actions	— Counsel	Prudence
		relative to worship	— Piety	(Religion) Justice
	the will and the sensitive appetites	against fear of danger	— Fortitude	Fortitude
		against disorderly concupiscences	— Fear	Temperance

What is the difference between the virtues and the gifts? The infused virtues, we know, are powers given to the soul which enable us to perform supernatural acts. These powers are "habits," abiding, not transitory, and we are always able to perform the acts toward which they direct us. The gifts have also been infused in us, but they are operative only at the will of the Holy Spirit. Returning to the example given by John of St. Thomas, we can always row a boat, but the sails are helpful only when there is a wind.

The virtues give us the ability to choose God as our object, to act with Him as our motive. The gifts are powerful aids to our doing so. For example, we have the power to love God because of charity, but an inspiration from the Holy Spirit whereby we have a strong

---

[11] Garrigou-Lagrange, O.P., *Christian Perfection and Contemplation* (St. Louis: B. Herder Book Co., 1939), p. 298.

and clear realization that God the Father is our Father (Piety) not only gives a different turn to our love but makes it immensely easier.

With the gifts the work is not all the Holy Spirit's. He takes the initiative and His inspiration, as we have indicated, makes the task of the will easier. The inspiration may have an effect on the body — feelings that older spiritual writers have called "consolations" — and this is a great help. But the final decision, to act on the inspiration or not, is up to us. True, the gifts make us more docile to the Holy Spirit, but this docility that has been infused must be accompanied by a docility on our part, lest we grieve the Holy Spirit.[12]

There is another difference between the virtues and the gifts, more difficult to understand, consisting in their mode of operation. When we act by the power of the infused virtues we still do so in a human manner. In our love that proceeds from charity we are loving with our human will in a way that is similar to human love. By faith we know the truths of Revelation, but through the human mode of intellection. Prudence enables the intellect to choose means to the beatific vision but by the ordinary processes of the intellect. Such is not the mode of operation of the gifts. The action of the Holy Spirit comes to us without any operation on our part. It is in the form of either intuitive knowledge or direct movements of the will. The relation of the truths of faith into some kind of synthesis is a laborious task for the intellect. By the gift of understanding the intellect can be given this

_____
[12] Cf. Eph. 4:30.

synthesis in a single inspiration. Prudence may seek the best way; counsel gives us the answer in an instant. The mode of operation of the gifts is therefore superhuman.[13]

While the subject matter is the same for both the virtues and the gifts, we can say that by the gifts we are able to see things as God sees them, whether the truths of faith, the persons and elements in our own life, or Himself. And we see them not only as they are, but in a unity, for God sees all in His own unity. "But to us God has revealed them through his Spirit, who fathoms all things, even the depths of God. Who among men knows the inner thoughts of a man save the man's spirit within him? Even so, the thoughts of God no one knows but the Spirit of God. Now we have received not the spirit of the world, but the spirit imparted by God. Thus we are enabled to recognize the gifts bestowed on us by God. These are just the things we express in words taught by the Spirit, not in words taught by human wisdom, when we make a synthesis of spiritual truths for the spiritually minded."[14]

Are the gifts only for great moments and crises? No, since we need them for our daily spiritual life. "There seems to be no reason for hesitation in asserting in this connection that every single act which is specifically an act of a child of God proceeds from the gifts. . . . We cannot act as children of God unless the Holy Ghost be at our side."[15]

---

[13] Cf. St. Thomas, *Commentary on the Book of Sentences,* III, d. 34, q. 1, a. 1.

[14] 1 Cor. 2:10–13.

[15] Bernard J. Kelly, C.S.Sp., *The Seven Gifts* (New York: Sheed & Ward, 1942), p. 24.

As we increase in docility to the Holy Spirit we shall live habitually by them and we shall let Him, God Himself, make us into Christ.

INDIVIDUAL PRACTICES

1. For a while say the *Veni, Sancte Spiritus* daily.
2. Honor the Holy Spirit in a special way each day.
3. Examine your life for evidence of the gifts.
4. Meditate on the operation of the infused virtues and the gifts in the course of one day.
5. Synthesize the book thus far.
6. Reread Christ's discourse and prayer after the Last Supper in the light of this chapter.

GROUP QUESTIONS AND ACTIVITIES

1. What is the relation between activity and passivity in living by the gifts?
2. Study the operation of the gifts in the life of the Founder.
3. Study the proper texts of the Pentecost Masses with reference to the gifts.
4. Study all the Epistles for references to the Holy Spirit.
5. Study the Gospels for references to Christ's relations with the Holy Spirit.
6. Present a paper on the influence of the gifts in the life of your patron.
7. Study the operation of the Holy Spirit in the lives of the men of God in the Old Testament.
8. Write a play with the virtues and gifts as characters, in the manner of the medieval morality plays.

CHAPTER 26

Fear of God

What I hope to achieve: *To understand and appreciate the gift of fear of God.*

In our study of humility and religion we learned that our fundamental spiritual attitude is a grasp of the relation between God and ourselves. Both virtues proceed from the realization that God is God and we are His creatures, that He is Being from Himself, we are being from Him, that He is necessary, we are contingent. It is a humbling realization, but one that gives us the right perspective from which to view God and men; it is practical, because from it flows our whole duty toward God: glory, which translates itself into adoration, love, service.

Two founders, St. Benedict and St. Ignatius, in the "spiritual exercises" for their beginners (the twelve degrees comprise St. Benedict's "spiritual exercises," his whole plan of asceticism), insist on this basic frame of mind. "The first degree of humility, then, is that a person always keeping the fear of God before his eyes should avoid all forgetfulness and be ever mindful of all that God has commanded, and of the fact that those who contemn God fall into hell for their sins;

that one should ever meditate in his heart on the everlasting life which has been prepared for those who fear God."[1] The first sentence of St. Ignatius' First Principle and Foundation reads: "Man was created to praise, reverence, and serve God our Lord. . . ."[2] And in the first exercise for the first week he enjoins the exercitant "to ask our Lord God for grace that all my intentions, actions, and operations may be ordained purely to the service and praise of His Divine Majesty."[3] Throughout the *Exercises* occur the words "praise," "serve," and "obey." St. Ignatius had been a soldier, and when he saw Christ as King and Commander, he was expressing in terms familiar to him and his followers the gap that exists between Christ and them. St. Benedict's first attitude is that of almost servile fear, but it develops into reverence and love. St. Ignatius' attitude is the devotion to the cause of the Leader, which devotion is compounded of respect and reverence, personal love and trust. It too is at base a fear but one that is more unselfish and devoted. But the point we are making here is that these two wise, holy, and successful founders have required of their followers this profound and constant understanding of the essential difference between God and man. On this they should build the superstructure of their spiritual life.

This is the reason why we begin our study of the individual gifts with that of fear of God. Humility is the foundation virtue, because it puts us in our proper

---

[1] St. Benedict, *Holy Rule*, pp. 27–28.

[2] St. Ignatius, *Spiritual Exercises*, no. 23.

[3] *Ibid.*, no. 46.

place before God and man, and fear is the fundamental gift, because by means of it the Holy Spirit can make us realize this proper place, and this realization is necessary for any further relations with Him. "The fear of the Lord is the beginning of wisdom."[4] This text we can interpret in the light of the gifts: our progress in union with God depends on our continued realization of the meaning of God.

Fear of God is the gift that enables us to receive from the Holy Spirit inspirations of fear of separation from Him and of our unworthiness of His majesty, perfection, and holiness. We distinguish two kinds of fear: servile and filial; the former is basically selfish, based on our desire to avoid punishment; the latter is other-directed and is founded on respect or love. Obviously, filial fear derives from the fundamental attitude of the child for its parent: an abiding realization of the position of each in relation to the other.

The fear that is the object of the gift is filial, for ". . . the gift cannot be based on servile fear which, although in itself it is not evil, can be found in a sinner."[5] The gift aims at elevating us above our selfish concern to God; it is supernatural in its end as well as in its operation. Fear is produced by an impending evil, and to the Christian the greatest evil is separation from God. The child dreads separation from his parents, and as he grows older the earlier fear develops into one of displeasing them, of separating himself from

---

[4] Ps. 110:10.

[5] John of St. Thomas, *The Gifts of the Holy Ghost* (London: Sheed and Ward, 1951), p. 198.

their love and esteem. When he has secured these he still fears losing their presence through death. These elements are present in our filial fear of God: the fear of separation from Him by sin, of displeasing Him, and, worst of all, of eternal loss of Him in the beatific vision. This fear, inspired by the Holy Spirit, has God, not self, for its motive; it is theocentric. Separation is dreaded because one realizes who and what God is — that He is to be adored, glorified, loved eternally, and that one has no other duty or object for existence. He grasps the fundamental relation of himself to God. What he fears is that he might not be able to tender God this eternal duty of glory.

He realizes, as a consequence of grasping who God is and who he is, his infinite unworthiness in contrast with God's being. He realizes God's perfection and his imperfection, God's holiness and his sinfulness. He knows now that he is, of himself, unworthy of the beatific vision. A good and wise son will come to similar conclusions about his position in relation to his parents'; he will at length appreciate not only their worth but also their necessity for his being.

When one realizes God, he understands sin, which is a deliberate rejection of Him as infinite Good; and, without any thought of self, he sees the injustice, the insanity, and the malice of such a rejection. Therefore he fears sin, not because of the punishment it will bring, but because of what it is in itself — an offense against God. The son who would not offend his parents because of their intrinsic worth has a similar attitude.

The person who lives by the operation of this gift

has a hatred of sin, which he sees as evil. He knows that only sin can separate him from God, that only sin displeases Him, and that his own past sins have increased his essential unworthiness of Him. Therefore he is most submissive to God's will, delicately attuned to it, aimed at perfect purity of heart. All in him must be restored to God, under rule of intellect and will. Hence, we see the relation between this gift and temperance.

However, its relation to religion is also obvious; the inspirations of fear are always realizations of the relation of God and self. And they also convince us that our happiness is not our primary ultimate end, but God's glory: we don't desire the beatific vision primarily so that we might be eternally happy. Rather we realize what the beatific vision is and desire it in order to give God eternal glory thereby, and understand that our eternal happiness is inseparable from this unending act.

INDIVIDUAL PRACTICES

1. Is the fear of God the basis of your spiritual life?
2. How could your troubles be solved if it were?
3. Is your fear of God more filial than servile?
4. Meditate on fear of God in Christ.
5. Meditate on the relation between the gift of fear and sin.
6. Meditate on the relation between the gift of fear and charity.
7. How does this gift help humility?

GROUP QUESTIONS AND ACTIVITIES

1. Study the Founder's writings as to his attitude toward the fear of God.
2. Discuss: The fear of the gift is filial, but you can never completely do away with servile fear.
3. Discuss: Devotion to Christ's humanity tends to lessen fear.
4. Write an essay on the fear of God in
   a) St. Bernard,
   b) St. Francis of Assisi,
   c) St. Francis de Sales,
   d) St. Margaret Mary, or
   e) St. Therese of Lisieux.
5. Discuss: The Liturgy fosters fear of God.
6. Let each present a psalm expressing fear of God.
7. Discuss: What is missing today is a *hatred* of sin.
8. Discuss in more detail the relation between fear and temperance, chastity, humility, and religion.

CHAPTER 27

Piety

What I hope to achieve: *To realize my state of adopted child of the Father and the relation of piety to it.*

God exercises a general fatherhood over all creation because He is the source. But He is the Father of the Christian in the unique sense of His being Father of His only-begotten Son. There is nothing metaphorical here: what the Son is by nature we who are one body with Him are by adoption. We are not mere foster children who do not bear the name nor have the legal rights of children. "God sent his Son . . . that we might receive the adoption. And because you are sons, God sent the Spirit of his Son into your hearts, crying, 'Abba, Father.' You are, then, no longer a slave but a son; and if a son, an heir also through God's grace."[1] "The decree that settled the Incarnation has settled everything in principle. It willed Christ alone; but in willing Him, it willed Him in His entirety, along with His fullness that is His mystical body. All things are divinely unified in these divine origins, and are the unified effect produced by the One; and the eternal predestination of the one Mediator between God and men, the man

[1] Gal. 4:4–7.

Jesus Christ, is so great and complete that it is also the predestination of all men who were to be His members."[2]

The work of the gift of piety is to create in us the mentality of sons. It equips us to receive those attitudes from the Holy Spirit that change our whole relationship with God. The fear of God that is the result of the gift is that of the son for his Father, but the emphasis is on the difference between Father and son. The gift of piety emphasizes family likeness. Both sets of attitudes balance and complement each other. Where realization of Creator and creature, awe and reverence, predominate in the gift of fear, the love of Christ for the Father, His Father-centered religion, predominate in that of piety.

Therefore, piety affects the virtue of religion. Of itself religion would regulate the individual adoration, worship, love, and service, which we rightfully owe to God as Supreme Being. Piety causes it to be the religion of Christ, the worshiper *par excellence*, because He is the Son and we are, in Him, sons. This religion, it is true, is that of the human nature adoring the Father, but the adoration is given by the Person of the Son. The sentiments of adoration, complete love, and giving of self, that Christ conveyed when He said the word "Father," the Holy Spirit will give us to a relative degree, because He cries in our hearts "Father." The virtue of religion regards God as a source; the gift of piety understands that source as Father.

[2] Mersch, *The Theology of the Mystical Body* (St. Louis: B. Herder Book Co., 1951), pp. 597–598.

By this gift we receive from the Holy Spirit inspirations regarding God as our Father that we would never conceive by our own intellect, because they seem to exceed what is reasonable. They go beyond what reason can know of God as Father and what it thinks to be proper, in their childlike daring and boldness. As a result, our attitude toward the Father becomes that of a little child who is too young and inexperienced to appreciate and fully understand his father's nature, personality, and position, who has no thought of consequences, who only knows that this man is his father who loves him. The great trust of St. Therese's "little way" was surely the result of such an inspiration. We shall always recognize a genuine inspiration deriving from the gift of piety because of the interaction of the whole complex of virtues and gifts. The inspiration will never oppose what we believe by faith, nor will it turn hope into presumption; the inspirations of the gift of fear of God will always provide a reverential basis, just as reverence for his father is always present to the child, at least subconsciously, in a good father-child relationship.

The inspirations of piety transform our love of God from that of a creature into that of a son, or if, as a result of our own meditation, we have been endeavoring to give Him this filial love, these inspirations can lift our love to a degree of filial love born of the conviction of experience. We know that we are sons. All of our relations with the Father henceforth have a filial character, for we know the truth, that He is our Father. Love is a joy, and hence our obedience and abandonment become acts not so much of reasoned love as of experienced love. With Christ we are able to say happily, in virtue of this love, ". . . at all times I do what is pleasing to him."[3]

Thus these inspirations will gradually give us the mentality of Christ as Son, the mentality that motivated His basic act of glory to the Father and redemption for man, His sacrificial obedience to the Father's will. Because of this mind of Christ which becomes ours, we view every element in our life, everything that we must do and suffer, as a means of giving the Father the sacrificial obedience of sons, for glory and redemption. With the mind of Christ we acquire a new perspective, the ability to see things as He sees and saw them, that all relate to this obedience, that all relate to the fact that God the Father is our Father and that we are in Christ His sons. Father and sons, there is the unifying synthesis of so much multiplicity in our life. To enable us to achieve this synthesis is the function of piety.

Piety ". . . looks upon men, not as men, but as sons of God, or as capable of being such. Worshipping God as Father, Piety sees all men as brothers by grace."[4] Everyone is at least a potential member of the Mystical Body, and the inspirations of piety give us a reverence for all men as being not mere creatures or what they are by nature and their own efforts, but sons of the Father. The term we use here is reverence, because of their great dignity, which so far exceeds any possible earthly dignity. Piety allows us to see a sacredness in

[3] Jn. 8:29.
[4] John of St. Thomas, *The Gifts of the Holy Ghost* (London: Sheed and Ward, 1951), pp. 185, 183.

each one, because he belongs to God not only as a creature but also as His own adopted son. Because of this reverence we respect the family rights of each other. "Blood is thicker than water" has always meant that family claims are the strongest. Thus piety transforms justice into a zeal for these claims.

We are reminded in this connection of Charles de Foucauld's designation of himself as "the universal brother," exemplified by his fraternal love of the nomad tribes of the Sahara. It could only have been an inspiration of piety that led the Little Brothers and the Little Sisters of Jesus, who are motivated by his spirit, to live and work with the very poor as witnesses to Christ's fraternal love, and therefore of their own, for these poor.

Our familial attitude must extend even beyond the human race and include the whole of God's creation. We must envision it as belonging to God who cares for it as a loving and provident Father. "Do not five sparrows sell for two pennies? And yet, in the providence of God, not one of them is a poor, forgotten creature! . . . Observe the ravens! They neither sow nor reap, nor have they storeroom or barn. God feeds them just the same."[5]

But creation belongs to the Son in a special way. "He is the image of the invisible God, the first-born of every creature, because in him were created all creatures in the heavens and on the earth, both visible and invisible, whether Thrones, or Dominations, or Principalities, or Powers. All have been created through him and for him. He exists prior to all creatures, and in him

---

[5] Lk. 12:6, 24.

they are all preserved in being."[6] The Son is the image of the Father, who gives Him all His being. Whatever has been created shares God's being and His perfection, is in some way an image of the divine image, who is then the exemplar of all that derives its being from the Creator-Father. All creation from its nature as creature partakes in a general way in the sonship of the Word. But the Word was joined to His creation in the hypostatic union which thereby consecrated creation to Him as His own. The Creator-Son in becoming a man — who is himself a microcosm, a composite of all the forms of creation — has taken His creatures into Himself by way of His human nature. The only Person of the Trinity who has a human nature, a created nature, is the Son. Therefore, creation leads us to the Son, reminds us of Him, and has, because of Him, a filial character. We can, with St. Francis of Assisi, call every creature our brother. But again we need the inspirations of piety to grasp this family attitude toward all creation, to reverence it as belonging in a special way to Christ.

We have so far only considered man and creation in general as partaking in the divine sonship. But piety will enable us to understand the special and deeper participation in God's fatherhood of the Holy Father and of those who share His authority or exercise it by His Vicar's approval. Its inspirations will make clear to us the special dedication of priests, religious, and consecrated laity to live out with perfect purity of heart their baptismal contract — the exchange of the life of the Son for their own.

---

[6] Col. 1:15–17.

We are re-created in the image of the Son. We must have His mind toward the Father and toward all creation, which is His brother. The Holy Spirit, who gives us the grace of adoption, gives us by the inspirations of piety this mind.

INDIVIDUAL PRACTICES

1. Read prayerfully the Epistle to the Ephesians in the light of this chapter.
2. Meditate on the divine adoption:
   a) That you must be the Son to the Father,
   b) That you are adopted sons, with the rights of sons.
3. Offer the Mass with Christ, joined to His attitude and sentiments as Son.
4. Live one day in the same attitude and sentiments.
5. Make Christ's prayer for unity after the Last Supper a subject for prayer.
6. Make the "Last Gospel" a subject for prayer.
7. Pray the *Veni, Sancte Spiritus* for the gift of piety.
8. For recollection, see others, and all objects which you use, as partaking in the divine sonship.

GROUP QUESTIONS AND ACTIVITIES

1. Discuss sanctifying grace, the virtues, and the gifts studied thus far in their function of making you into the Son.
2. How does the fact that you must be the Son to the Father unify your life, as it did and does Christ's?
3. Discuss in detail the effect of the gift of piety on your relations with the other community members.

4. How will the adoption of sons affect your apostolate? your other works of obedience?

5. Collect all the allusions of St. Paul to the adoption of sons.

6. Write a meditation on the Father-centered religion of Christ.

7. Discuss what has been written in this chapter in relation to distractions, to dissipation.

8. Discuss obedience as the sacrificial obedience of the incarnate Son.

CHAPTER 28

Fortitude

What I hope to achieve: *To appreciate and rely on the strength that is the result of this gift.*

Our immediate end is to become conformed to the image of the Son,[1] to "put on the Lord Jesus Christ."[2] We share in the divine nature, we are organically united to the Son, we have the infused virtues and other actual graces, but it is still a difficult process. The Holy Spirit must take us in hand, and when we yield ourselves to Him all goes well. "Whoever are led by the Spirit of God, they are the sons of God."[3]

The pursuit of moral good, our experience has taught us, is arduous, even with the help of the virtue of fortitude. Self is so hardy, so unwilling to give way to Christ. It is, at times, difficult to motivate ourselves with the thought of our end and our means. There are days, dry or tumultuous with temptations, when it seems as if we are incapable of thinking one fortifying thought. We need to say, *Veni, Sancte Spiritus!* For by the gift of fortitude, He gives us strengthening thoughts and can

---

[1] Cf. Rom. 8:29.
[2] Rom. 13:14.
[3] Rom. 8:14.

sweep our wills along with motivation. We are not alone in our times of need, and we know it. We know that we are united with our Head and with the whole Mystical Body, but what is going to give our weak wills that final push is the *realization* of this union and of its strength. This is the work of the Holy Spirit, realization and push, in His operations through this gift.

The virtue of fortitude strengthens our will, but the use of this virtue depends on us. Through the gift of fortitude the Holy Spirit Himself acts on us. True, our co-operation is needed if we are to act on the impulses of the Holy Spirit; we are able to resist Him. Yet the difference here lies in the fact that the virtue gives us ability, but the gift gives us God, who more or less takes over. Something similar occurs at the time of an approaching wedding, when the bride's parents are faced with the staggering task of preparation for the social side of the event. They are perfectly capable but they don't look forward to the work, the many details. Then a relative or friend who has had experience in "handling" a wedding steps in and offers to supervise the preparations. She takes the initiative, "bosses" the operations, keeps everything in motion. The parents are happy to be told what to do, while the experienced one masterminds the whole procedure.

It is necessary, therefore, that the gift mastermind the virtue, or, to be more correct, that the Holy Spirit direct our operation by the virtue of fortitude. The Holy Spirit and we, gift and virtue, co-operate daily, all through the day. We must prepare ourselves for this tremendous outside assistance by ever greater union of our will with the Father's and by letting Christ live in and through us more and more. Of course, all of this is impossible without the operations of the gifts; hence the need for us to be extremely docile to every movement of the Holy Spirit. And we must pray frequently for His coming, that He who conceived Christ's human nature in Mary, and His life in us in Baptism, may cause it to grow in us.

It is by this gift especially that the Holy Spirit moves our will to action, or inaction, as the case may be. The will normally moves when the intellect presents an object to it as good or as evil. But there are times when we feel that we should do or not do something, and we can perceive no reason for it. The Holy Spirit may be at work. It would be good to review St. Ignatius' rules for the discernment of spirits at this point.

It is at the time of martyrdom that the operation of the gift is markedly noticeable. St. Stephen, "filled with the Holy Spirit, looked up to heaven and saw the glory of God, and Jesus standing at the right hand of God."[4] This is the essential source of strength of the martyr, "the spirit of most burning love for our Lord Jesus Christ, who leads those animated by this spirit to do all and suffer all for love of Him, who did and suffered all for them."[5]

In the authentic acts of the early martyrs we read with wonder at the calm joy with which they endured the most cruel tortures. In the account of the martyr-

---

[4] Acts 7:55.
[5] St. John Eudes, The Kingdom of Grace (New York: P. J. Kenedy & Sons, 1954), p. 97.

dom of St. Polycarp occurs this typical passage: "Those martyrdoms are blessed and noble, then, which take place according to the will of God, for we must be careful to ascribe to God the power over all occurrences. For everyone surely marvels at their nobility and patience and love of the Lord. For, when they were so torn by whips that the structure of their flesh was visible even to the inner veins and arteries, they endured, so that even the bystanders pitied them and wept; while some of them attained such a degree of heroism that they neither groaned nor cried, thus showing all of us that at the time of their torture the noble martyrs of Christ were absent from the flesh, or rather that the Lord stood by and spoke to them. Because they kept in mind the grace of Christ, they despised the tortures of the world, thus purchasing eternal life at the price of a single hour . . . with the eyes of their heart they looked up to the good things which are stored up for those who have persevered. . . . This they were shown by the Lord, for they were no longer men, but already angels."[6]

In this passage we can see parallels with our own life, in which there have been and will be occasions when we feel as if we were being "so torn by whips" "even to the inner veins and arteries." Fortitude, virtue and gift for martyrdom, equips us for the martyrdom of the ordinary spiritual life, for perseverance therein, a martyrdom perhaps more glorious in that it is won, not "at the price of a single hour," but of a whole life.

Fortitude helps us to die well, as Christians. It takes

---

[6] "The Martyrdom of St. Polycarp," in *The Apostolic Fathers* (New York: Cima Publishing Co., Inc., 1947), pp. 151–152.

special strength to face this separation of the two essential parts of our human nature, but the gift can make it possible for us to go not only bravely but also eagerly to our death because of a conviction such as St. Paul had: "For me to live means Christ and to die means gain."[7]

The twelfth-century Cistercian abbot, Adam of Perseigne, wrote of the gifts as "seven silences, which by their own authority impose silence on all vices; which silences . . . permit the ears of the heart to hear the mysteries of the Incarnate Word." Later in the same passage he assigns the work of silencing the vices to the gift of fortitude, "Only by the Spirit of Fortitude are the vices silenced. . . ."[8]

This is a valid and practical view of the gift. We are unable to hear the Holy Spirit because of the clamor of the passions, of self demanding to be obeyed. Fortitude, like a good and firm disciplinarian, gets that interior silence so that we can hear Him giving us the mind of the Word.

INDIVIDUAL PRACTICES

1. Precisely how is self opposing becoming another Christ?
2. Examine in general several past temptations and see how you didn't make use of all the supernatural helps; how you should have.

---

[7] Phil. 1:21.

[8] ML, CCXI, col. 689c. I am indebted to Fr. Louis Merton's manuscript conference notes for the reference to Adam of Perseigne.

3. Live one day sensitive to the operation of the gift of fortitude.

4. Meditate on fortitude in Christ's Passion and Death.

5. Meditate on the necessity of fortitude for perseverance in the religious life.

GROUP QUESTIONS AND ACTIVITIES

1. Study the battle between self and Christ in the life of the Founder.

2. Compose a composite Stations of the Cross combining the elements of fear, piety, and fortitude.

3. Discuss the relation between natural love and natural fortitude, charity and fortitude.

4. Discuss the place of fortitude in the apostolate today.

5. Collect texts from the Masses of martyrs relative to fortitude.

CHAPTER 29

Counsel

> **What I hope to achieve:** *To value and make use of the inspirations of the Holy Spirit which come to me because of this gift.*

Counsel is the gift of inspiration for great works and great decisions in the apostolate. The founders of religious communities and innovators in the Church were prompted by its operation. Turning points in the spiritual life have been its work, but it is active even in the smallest decisions of the most unnoticed, of persons who have done nothing but the ordinary things.

By the virtue of prudence we are enabled to decide the best means, to take the right step, or to remain inactive. But prudence is difficult to exercise, and the gift of counsel comes to the aid of the intellect, still wondering and wavering, admitting the clear light of inspiration, which marks the decision as right. Or else, when prudence has done its best, and because of natural confusion the intellect cannot see a decision, inspiration gives what the Holy Spirit wills. Lallement wrote of it, "It is a light by which the Holy Spirit shows what we ought to do in the time, place and circumstances in which we find ourselves. What faith, wisdom, and knowledge teach in general, the gift of counsel applies to particular cases."[1] Therefore, by counsel we receive the inspirations that show us what is God's will for us here and now. It is concerned not with generalities but particulars, not with principles in general but their practical application in a given instance. By it we know good from bad, better from good. Something may be better in itself, but not for us. By counsel we know what to do.

We have stated that through this gift great and new works have been done in the Church. St. Francis was thus enlightened as to the entirely new form of life which he originated. At first, it is true, he did not intend to found an Order, but to start a movement, a movement in fact, of poor, humble men, tramping through Italy in two's, in imitation of the disciples, preaching the Gospel simply and joyfully. The inspiration for this innovation in the life of the Church, this return to the very spirit and circumstances of Christ's preaching, must have come from the Holy Spirit. When the movement developed into an Order, the latter itself was an innovation, breaking with the monastic way of life and even with the canonical. The other mendicant Orders would resemble those of the canons regular, but the Franciscans were to preserve in their spirit the elements of St. Francis' originality. Père de Clorivière originated an even greater departure from traditional religious life when he set the pattern for secular institutes in 1790 with his Daughters of the Heart of Mary.

---

[1] Lallement, *Spiritual Doctrine* (Westminster, Md.: The Newman Bookshop, 1947), p. 147.

Only in 1947 did the Church establish as a true canonical state of perfection the life of lay persons dedicated to God by private consecration and devoted to the apostolate, living in the world. Père de Clorivière had seen the validity of such a life, and although the Church approved his Society as a religious congregation, his inspiration was a precedent for the later development. "The Holy Spirit made known to me the necessity of taking a somewhat different way . . . in order to bring the world back to sound principles. Its members wear the same dress and submit to the same laws and customs as ordinary people, in so far as these are in accordance with the law of the Holy Gospel, accepting all the obligations of civil life and not upsetting in any way the order of public or family life."[2] St. Vincent de Paul's idea for the Daughters of Charity was a departure that could only have been inspired. And so, to mention only a few, were the bold concepts of St. Ignatius, the synthesis of monasticism with scholarly defense of truth of St. Dominic, and the dream of Charles de Foucauld of the Order he was never able to found.

We read in the lives of saints and saintly persons of their frequent prayers for light when forced to make some great decision, of their urging others to pray for this intention. They were praying to the Holy Spirit to act on them through the gift of counsel. To direct supplication were added fasting and vigils, thereby teaching us that such great grace — which the Holy Spirit can and does give without our asking — should

---

[2] From material supplied by the Daughters of the Heart of Mary, New York City, p. 7.

be asked of Him, with the intensity of adoration, trust, and abandonment. It is not without reason that in the Church so many decisive ceremonies begin with the *Veni, Creator.*

But while counsel is necessary for the great moments in the history of the Church as well as in individual lives, it is equally necessary for the small moments. "All the elect do have the gift of counsel. They may not have it in its higher form nor in the direction and judgment of natural and temporal matters. However, they have it concerning anything necessary for salvation, and for the disdain of temporal things lest they hinder and divert a man from celestial things."[3] There are times of real perplexities, when obedience leaves us free and consultation has resulted in no decision. Then we need to say with the intensity of the saints, *Veni, Sancte Spiritus!*

We have mentioned consultation. May we ask advice in our doubts, or is this grieving the Spirit, who alone is capable to advise? John of St. Thomas quotes St. John's first epistle: ". . . test the spirits to see whether they are of God, . . ."[4] adding, "Ordinarily this examination and test should be done with the consultation and advice of others, since ordinarily the illumination of God is given with concomitant dependence upon others, inferiors being enlightened by superiors."[5]

"It is true," he writes later, "that sometimes even

[3] John of St. Thomas, *The Gifts of the Holy Ghost* (London: Sheed and Ward, 1951), p. 164.

[4] 1 Jn. 4:1 (Conf. ed.).

[5] John of St. Thomas, *op. cit.*, p. 168.

without consultation the Holy Ghost moves men to a course of action surpassing human prudence."[6] But we shall always know whether it is the Holy Spirit who speaks, or self, or the devil, by checking the inspiration with obedience. "We are born of God," wrote St. John the Evangelist of the Church. "He who knows God listens to us; he who is not born of God does not listen to us. By this test we distinguish the spiritual manifestation that is inspired by the truth from the spiritual manifestation that is inspired by the deceiver."[7] How many mistakes and schisms in the religious life, how many deluding "inspirations," would have been avoided if only those in question had listened to the Church giving the mind of the Holy Spirit through obedience.

It stands to reason that in the silence of purity of heart we shall hear the Holy Spirit best, when the noise of the passions and the insistent demands of self have been relatively stilled. We need His inspirations for guidance, but only those who are habitually obedient and abandoned to His will and direction are most likely not only to hear, but also to recognize His voice.

Grace builds on nature, an axiom we must never forget. Lallement has taught that the combination of love of God and natural common sense is a good foundation for the successful functioning of counsel: "A person of good sound judgment, who should study constantly purity of heart, would acquire a supernatural prudence and a divine skill in conducting all sorts of affairs, would receive an abundance of infused light and knowledge for the guidance of souls, and discover a thousand holy

---

[6] *Ibid.*, p. 169.   [7] 1 Jn. 4:6.

contrivances for the execution of enterprises which concern the glory of God. . . . It was by purity of heart, and by a faithful reliance on the guidance of the Holy Spirit, that St. Ignatius and St. Francis Xavier acquired that rare gift of prudence for which they have been admired."[8]

INDIVIDUAL PRACTICES

1. Examine your life as to the operation in it of this gift and your correspondence to it.
2. Do you readily ask for advice?
3. Are you habitually indecisive? Ask for advice too frequently?
4. Do you "check" on inspirations with your director, superior?
5. Form the habit of asking the Holy Spirit for the operation of counsel, for inspirations according to the gift.
6. Meditate on this gift in Christ's life.

GROUP QUESTIONS AND ACTIVITIES

1. Study the work of counsel in the Founder's life.
2. Study it in the history of the community.
3. What is the relation between natural common sense and counsel?
4. What are some "success stories" in the lives of saints and saintly persons, the apparent result of counsel? What are some failures, obviously not the result? What was the role of Church authority in all of these?
5. How should a spiritual director use this gift? How should a superior?

---

[8] Lallement, *op. cit.*, p. 149.

CHAPTER 30

Knowledge

What I hope to achieve: *To understand the operation of this gift, and by it come to understand creation.*

"And this good pleasure he [the Father] decreed to put into effect in Christ when the designated period of time had elapsed, namely to gather all creation, both in heaven and on earth under one head, Christ."[1] All creation is to be reheaded in Christ, to be taken in some way into the whole Christ. But what is this way? St. Paul has also indicated the method: "For all things belong to you, whether . . . the world, or life, or death, or the present, or the future. All things belong to you, and you to Christ, and Christ to God."[2] Creation is taken into Christ through us, through our use of it. "God did not send the Son into the world to condemn the world. Not at all; the world is to be saved through him."[3] It is saved when we use it as Christ intends us to, or rather, as Christ wills to use it through us. Because we love Christ we unite our will with His; and, in our love and primarily because of Him, we make

[1] Eph. 1:10.
[2] 1 Cor. 3:22–23.
[3] Jn. 3:17.

creation ours. But there is no danger because we are Christ's. Creation does not exist for us, we are not its end, because we are not our own end. The Father, not self, is the term, as He is the source, of creation.

The Father has given us creation out of love, and lovingly we use it, as the Son, the first born of creation. Thus does the redemption come to it. "All creation awaits with eager longing the manifestation of the sons of God."[4] The unity willed by the Father in willing the Incarnation is accomplished: even the diverse and most minute elements of His creation are taken into the unity of the whole Christ by the action of Christ through His members, by our use and enjoyment of them as adopted sons. "It is ever through him that all these good gifts, created so by thee, Lord, are by thee sanctified, endowed with life, blessed, and bestowed upon us."[5] All are ours and we are Christ's and Christ is the Father's!

It is to give us this vision of creation, to widen and deepen it, that the Father has given us the gift of knowledge. By it the Holy Spirit enlightens us with true understanding of creation and its meaning: its necessary relation to God. As we have seen, creation does not exist for itself, nor for us, but for us in Christ, and, ultimately, for the Father. The gift allows us to receive the Father's knowledge of creation. Hence we receive a unified view of everything and everyone.

Because of this view we see creation in terms of the

[4] Rom. 8:19.
[5] Canon of the Mass, *The Missal* (Westminster: The Newman Press, 1958).

Creator. Each created being speaks to us of its uncreated Cause. "Since the creation of the world his invisible attributes are clearly seen — especially his everlasting power and divinity, which are understood through the things that are made."[6] If this is true of natural knowledge, what must the knowledge of the gift tell us of God "through the things that are made"?

Through knowledge we know ourselves, our state of soul, and our particular needs. Counsel is concerned with making decisions, based on the condition that knowledge has disclosed. "The judgment of knowledge is not purely practical. It is speculative and resolves things to their causes. Therefore, it is not immediately and precisely concerned with actions, as is the case with prudence and counsel."[7]

Knowledge is, then, necessary for our safe guidance of others, for by it we are able to know their spiritual condition, strong points and weaknesses, as well as precisely what in their make-up is most receptive and to what approach. Therefore, superiors, preachers, spiritual directors, and teachers need knowledge constantly and in abundance. To move the will — we know from our own life how difficult that is. And to move a number of wills, each individual, in a context of impressions whose synthesis is individual, is no task for the purely natural. How those whose work it is to so move need to beg the Holy Spirit for the knowledge that only comes from Him, daily, frequently!

---

[6] Rom. 1:20.

[7] John of St. Thomas, *The Gifts of the Holy Ghost* (London: Sheed and Ward, 1951), p. 152.

Knowledge especially aids hope, for it is opposed to materialism. Matter is essentially finite, hence can never perfectly satisfy desire which, knowingly or unknowingly, is seeking the infinite. Besides this basic shortcoming, matter is corruptible. Therefore materialism — seeking matter for itself — is frustrating and ends in pessimism. The materialist has no hope, only the assurance of the poverty and corruption of his object. Knowledge shows us that beyond the material is God — eternal, unbounded, unchanging — and that by means of creation we go to Him.

Thus related to hope, knowledge facilitates our abandonment. The Holy Spirit can show us that this circumstance is from God, gives Him to us, and is His way, here and now, of forming us into Christ. We know all this in general and in theory, but what we need so often is to know it in fact, to *realize* it.

We have stated elsewhere that true detachment is attachment to others and detachment from self. Knowledge will give us this twofold process. We must love creation. Only by our love of it can *it* be redeemed, and feel the effects of Christ's mediation. He touches His creation through our contacts, loves it through our love. By our respect and love for it we take it into the Mystical Body, not, of course, in its physical being, but in its effect of helping us to give God glory. Our love of creation is safe if we realize that all are ours and we are Christ's, if we are primarily, essentially, and, if He would demand it, totally, attached to Him. The gift of knowledge can give us this Christian detachment by the vision it allows us, true and unified, of creation.

This synthesis of God and His work which is the special work of this gift will cause us "to diminish the contrast between 'God' and the 'World' which is doing so much harm to Christianity today. The Popes have been inciting us for more than fifty years to eradicate this deep antithesis which divides the world of thought, and they have been urging us towards a reconstruction of society and normal life, because the division between 'God' and 'Things' is one of the most important factors which go to explain that repugnance towards religion which so many men seem to have."[8]

If man is a union of all the forms of creation, a miniature cosmos, spiritual and material, so is Christ. Creation is joined to the Creator in Him. Matter was consecrated by the Incarnation.

Therefore the gift gives a great impetus to the virtue of religion, for everything in the universe is sacred to God, not only because God created it, is present in it, and owns it, but also because it is destined for Christ, the beloved Son. Creation belongs to Him in a special way since He is its first born, and nature "groans and travails" until it is reheaded in Him.

Knowledge gives the true sense of humor, a vital requisite for an integral and balanced spiritual, hence religious, life. "Without it, the enclosure can easily become a spiritual hothouse where every trifle marks a crisis, and pettiness grows into a cult." The "old maid" has no sense of humor. "In point of fact, it is a thing rooted in the Divine, for a real sense of humor is what

---

[8] Gustave Thils, *Christian Attitudes* (Dublin: Scepter, 1959), pp. 94–95.

balances the mysteries of joy and sorrow. Without it, we can never hold a true perspective on ourselves or on others. The saints were the true humorists. The better poets were humorists. The ability to see *through* things and to know what is important and what is not, what is to be endured and why we endure it, what is to be tolerated out of compassion and what is to be extirpated out of duty, is dependent upon one's sense of humor. Without the one, we cannot possess the other."[9] The sense of humor is the ability to recognize the incongruous. Taking ourselves seriously is incongruous, since we are important to the Father only in our likeness to the Son. Humor is based on humility, and the recognition of ourself in relation to God is given to us by knowledge.

INDIVIDUAL PRACTICES

1. Examine yourself as to your habitual attitude toward creation.
2. Take a meditative walk and see creation as related to God. Be conscious that you are taking it into the whole Christ.
3. In the Office realize that all creation is praising God through you, especially in the *Benedicite* and Psalms 148–150.
4. Meditate on St. Francis' Canticle of the Sun.
5. Meditate on your need for a sense of humor.
6. Offer creation to the Father in the Mass in the Person of the God-Man.

---

[9] Sister Mary Francis, P.C., *A Right to be Merry* (New York: Sheed & Ward, 1956), pp. 37–38.

7. Examine yourself as to your abandonment to God's will.

GROUP QUESTIONS AND ACTIVITIES

1. Study the references of Christ to creation.
2. What is the attitude of the Rule and Constitutions?
3. How could a person rationalize and become lax, self-indulgent, and worldly, in loving creation?
4. How can loving creation help you keep your balance?
5. Consider the difference in *loving* creation — persons and things, and *depending* on creation for happiness. What would be the dangers in the first which could lead to the second?
6. Read aloud some poems that (a) express a love of creation, or (b) see creation in relation to God.
7. Discuss poetry, satire, as proceeding from the sense of humor.

CHAPTER 31

Understanding

What I hope to achieve: *To appreciate the need faith has for the inspirations by this gift.*

Through fear of God we realize our fundamental relation to Him, through piety we determine to live our sonship, through fortitude we are able to do so, and through knowledge we realize the relation of the rest of creation to that sonship.

The field of understanding is revealed truth, its credibility and meaning. Through this gift, therefore, we are given the mind of the Father as to what He has told us through Christ. "You are privileged to know the mysteries of the kingdom of heaven. . . ."[1] The gift of knowledge gives us His mind with regard to creation, but that of understanding allows us glimpses into His own truth, the truth of His being. For all revelation is revelation of God. What we are attempting by means of this gift is in some way to understand God.

But revelation is clothed in symbols, first in the symbols of words. "Now there are many kinds of things

---

[1] Mt. 13:11.

that are hidden within, to find which human knowledge has to penetrate within so to speak. . . . Since, however, human knowledge begins with the outside of things as it were, it is evident that the stronger the light of the understanding, the further can it penetrate into the heart of things."[2] But the human understanding is unable to penetrate through the symbols to the heart of revelation. Only the gift can make this possible.

In our times when there has been a great return to dogma and its sources, Scripture studies have not only revived but have adopted a scientific method never before possible. Translations are as accurate as biblical scholarship and skill in biblical languages can achieve, and exegesis is concerned with the most literal of interpretations in the most accurate contexts. How fortunate we are to have these treasures. What a basis for the operation of understanding! We read the word of God reverently, lovingly, tasting the meaning. We turn it into prayer, and we ask the Holy Spirit to give us the penetration "into the heart of things," that is understanding.

The word, we know from Christ's telling us, is a seed — "the seed is the word of God."[3] But the seed sprouts and grows without our knowing it,[4] deep in our unconscious. Tended by the Holy Spirit it becomes fruitful and nourishes our charity. At times we notice it, or it flashes upon our conscious intellect with a depth of meaning that can only be the result of the gift. Many

---

[2] *Summa Theologica*, II–II, q. 8, a. 1.
[3] Lk. 8:11 (Conf. tr.).
[4] Cf. Mk. 4:27.

a Scripture text carefully remembered and then planted is finally understood in this way.

Or else during the course of a liturgical act, when the context of other texts and the sensory aids of music, color, and movement have provided a natural foundation for it, understanding will reveal the true meaning of a word of God.

Understanding is concerned not only with the meaning of revelation but also with its credibility. We are still in the way of faith, yet the Holy Spirit demonstrates to us that the truths of faith are eminently worthy of belief. His action is conviction, without removing the necessity of belief.

Primarily speculative, understanding permits us to receive from the Holy Spirit certain consequences of revealed truth that have a bearing on practical life. Such a consequence would be the mystical life of Christ in His members. The Mystical Body is a dogma, but the wonderful effect of this dogma — that Christ is reliving His earthly life, especially His interior — that has to be told us, not only in general but in its particulars, by the Holy Spirit. Only then can we more fully understand the dogma.

By understanding we receive insights into the sacraments. The Holy Spirit will be active in our preparation for their reception; His inspiration will make their reception joyful and their effects fruitful. How different the Mass and Office as liturgical acts can be because of this gift.

We know something either by word or by experience, either by reading and hearing or by living. The former method is speculative, theoretical, and the second, practical, experimental. How do we know through the gift of understanding? Essentially our knowledge so received is by experience, for the Holy Spirit gives an idea or ideas directly to our intellect, which then become translated into words. He does not "speak." He communicates knowledge, which process gives us an experience of His knowledge.[5]

Understanding is the gift that aids, strengthens, our faith, for whereas faith accepts on the authority of God, understanding enables us to realize the truth of faith by bringing us into a lived contact with God. The man who lives by this gift has no need of apologetics: he is almost in the position of a witness who has "been there and knows."

But what purity of heart the operation of understanding demands, what a silence of the passions. And what a loss of possible inspirations, which could not only radically change us but make our lives easier and joyful, for us religious with our daily Scripture reading, liturgy, and prayer. We are in daily contact with Scripture, but are we in daily contact with the Spirit of understanding?

INDIVIDUAL PRACTICES

1. Always beg the Holy Spirit to make His gift operative in you before your daily Scripture reading.
2. Begin the habit of letting Scripture reading develop into prayer.

[5] Cf. John of St. Thomas, The Gifts of the Holy Ghost (London: Sheed and Ward, 1951), p. 99.

3. Memorize one Scripture text a day and recall it from time to time.

4. Change Scripture translations from time to time.

5. Be attentive to the interpretation given the Scripture texts of the Propers of the Mass and Office by their liturgical use.

6. When you have time, read one of the Epistles straight through.

7. For a while read a good commentary on the Psalms for spiritual reading, e.g., St. Augustine's.

GROUP QUESTIONS AND ACTIVITIES

1. Discuss the merits of the different translations of Scripture.

2. Write essays on recent developments in Scripture study.

3. Study the operation of this gift in the life of Abbot Marmion, what he calls "lights."

4. Study the different meanings in Scripture.

5. Give instances from the lives of saints of understanding giving them "proof" for the truths of revelation.

6. Relate the leading ideas of the Old Testament with the New Testament.

CHAPTER 32

Wisdom

What I hope to achieve: *To understand the role of wisdom in my union with God.*

Why do we say that a certain man is wise? It is because he always knows why. The philosopher, whom we usually associate with the virtue of wisdom, is not primarily concerned with effects but with causes, the why of things. He who knows causes is wise, and he who has pushed back to the Ultimate Cause is wisest of all.

Hence the gift of wisdom is concerned with the Ultimate Cause, the divine Why, not known in Its effects, but in Itself. The gift makes us capable of experiencing God, and in this experience of realizing that everything proceeds from Him as its Cause.[1]

We may know everything about God that is humanly possible to know, and yet not know God. We may receive Christ in daily Communion and have never experienced Him. Wisdom gives us this encounter, this experimental knowledge. It may be very brief, last for a while, or even be habitual, but we are never the same after it happens for, in a way adapted to our present state of faith, we have "seen" God.

[1] Cf. John of St. Thomas, *The Gifts of the Holy Ghost* (London: Sheed and Ward, 1951), pp. 125, 142.

This experimental knowledge is essentially a simple insight into God, which may be vivid and striking, or even unperceived. It may have the form of an awareness of God's presence, or a "light" as to His being, or one of His attributes; it may result in understanding a truth of revelation or of creation. Wisdom differs from understanding in that by wisdom we know revelation from knowing God; we proceed from Infinite Truth to revealed truth. The "simple insight into God" allows us to know somewhat as He knows, and, in the unity of His knowledge which sees all whole because in Himself, we are able to apprehend dogmas whole, "no longer separately seen in their customary statement: for they are no longer dispersed in verbal formulas but brought together in the unique focus of the eternal Light; they are perceived in God, in the very life that they enunciate and of which they are some beginning in us. . . ."[2] So wisdom differs from knowledge, which proceeds from creature to Creator. Wisdom shows us creatures in the Creator; we see them in Him. Knowing Him, the Source, in this way, we know His effects.

The Son is Wisdom, for He not only knows the Source, but is this knowledge, and expresses it in His eternal state of Word.[3] "Christ, the power of God and the wisdom of God."[4] The Holy Spirit gives us by means of this gift contact with Christ by which He is experimentally perceived as Wisdom, the Word. "Real divine love springs from the fatherly Heart when God

[2] Maurice Zundel, *Our Lady of Wisdom* (New York: Sheed & Ward, 1940), p. 32.
[3] Cf. Wisd. 7:25; Prov. 8:27–30.
[4] 1 Cor. 1:24.

utters His eternal Word in the soul. In this conversation the love of the Holy Spirit overflows and floods the soul and all its faculties so that everything that flows from her is love. This brings the senses under the control of the inner man, silencing their powers, while the inner love burns in God. Thus the soul expands and the eternal Word from which perfect love issues, is spoken."[5] The highest and closest union possible in this life with the Son, and in Him, with the Father, is effected by the gift of wisdom.

We realize, therefore, that the operation of the gift not only affects the intellect but also the will. While the latter is still free, yet the force of the experience in the intellect, the deep perception of God as highest Good, act on it as a determinant. There can be a bodily reaction, too, in the emotions, in evoking certain ones and suppressing others.

Faith is perfected by wisdom, for what the former believes the latter experiences, although still leaving us in the realm of faith. What we receive by the gift is experimental knowledge of God, infused knowledge, above and beyond reason and simple adherence to revealed truth. The Latin word for wisdom is *sapientia*, from the verb *sapere*, "to taste."

Wisdom, the experience of the eternal Wisdom, is the fulfillment of charity. Charity is union with God, wisdom is the enjoyment of that union by experimental contact. Charity lives on faith, but after the coming of wisdom it is sustained by faith realized. The presence

---

[5] C. F. Kelley, ed., *The Book of the Poor in Spirit* (New York: Harper and Brothers, 1954), pp. 260–261.

of God is believed by charity, but known, however obscurely, by wisdom. Charity loves, but wisdom possesses.

The perception of God by wisdom may not be consciously realized at all. "His dazzling light produces darkness in the intellect not adapted to receive it; His strength overwhelms human weakness," writes Père Marie-Eugène, O.C.D. "God can infuse into a soul His sublimest favors without the soul's being experimentally conscious of receiving them. . . . Saint Teresa speaks of very great lights she discovered in her soul without knowing exactly when she received them."[6] But the Spirit breathes as He will, and His presence may be acutely felt. When it is, a complete and utter realization of one's nothingness must be an accompaniment: "God is that which is, the creature is that which is not!" The visitations of God are always known by their results.

Although, in our study of the gifts, we have assigned particular effects to each one, this has only been for the sake of clarity. We are, in the matter of the gifts, in the presence of a mystery, the free action upon us of the Holy Spirit, who is not bound. He will breathe where and as He will. Effects which the theology of the gifts declares to be proper to one gift He can give with those of another. It is all *His* action. We must be humble, pure of heart, docile, and, in the last analysis, pray simply, *Veni, Sancte Spiritus!*

What we have considered so far in this chapter has been *acts*, as it were, produced by the Holy Spirit in us by means of the gift, isolated visitations. But there

---

[6] *Op. cit.*, pp. 353, 352.

is a condition which can be called the state of wisdom, in which this visitation becomes an abiding, and this is the contemplative state. We distinguish here between contemplative state and contemplative life: the latter is a life ordered and conditioned to the former, a favorable climate for it, such as that of the cloistered orders; the state is infused contemplation as the permanent action on the soul of, primarily, wisdom, understanding, and charity.

Infused contemplation, wrote the Doctor of Mystical Theology, St. John of the Cross, ". . . is an infused and loving knowledge of God, which enlightens the soul and at the same time enkindles it with love, until it is raised up step by step, even unto God its Creator."[7]

"St. Thomas, in conformity with tradition, teaches that contemplation is chiefly the fruit of the gift of wisdom. . . . But as the gift of wisdom presupposes charity, contemplation depends essentially also on charity, which makes us desire to know God better, not for the joy of knowing, but for God Himself, that we may love Him more."[8] "The necessary and also preponderant role of the gifts of the Holy Spirit, especially of Wisdom and Understanding, can be considered to be a certain doctrine. Without interior perfecting of living faith, without this passive actualisation of the gifts by the special inspirations of the Holy Spirit . . . one cannot see how infused contemplation would be theologically intelligible."[9]

[7] E. Allison Peers, tr., The Complete Works of St. John of the Cross (Westminster: The Newman Press, 1949), p. 462.
[8] Garrigou-Lagrange, O.P., Christian Perfection and Contemplation (St. Louis: B. Herder Book Co., 1939), pp. 313–314.
[9] Dictionnaire de Spiritualité, fasc. XV, col. 2192.

Infused contemplation is the full development of sanctifying grace, the virtues, and the gifts. Since the gifts perfect the virtues, contemplation is a part of this process.

St. John describes it as infused knowledge of God; hence it is a simple "gaze." There are stages in the contemplative state, but all can be described in saying that the contemplative process is the ever deeper realization of God present in the soul — which realization is given by the Holy Spirit — and the successive possession by Him of the whole person: will, intellect, imagination, body. This knowledge is "loving" because from the beginning of contemplation the Holy Spirit captivates the will, even when the intellect is unable to perceive the knowledge, deep within the soul. This grace cannot be merited, it is a gift. We have the "equipment," also a gift, but we can no more expect it by right than we can produce it. All we can do is prepare by living by the virtues and the gifts. "Very numerous are they who view the promised land from a distance, but never enter it on account of their infidelities."[10]

The contemplative state is and presupposes more than prayer. It is a whole way of life, influencing every facet of life. It is true, of its essence it is prayer, but its effects are too wide to conceive of it as another process of prayer: the development of the virtues under the influence of the gifts. As such it is in the normal development of the Christian life.

---

[10] Dom Vital Lehodey, O.C.S.O., *The Ways of Mental Prayer* (Dublin: M. H. Gill and Son., Ltd., 1951), p. 228. **An excellent guide.**

St. John of the Cross has given definite indications as to when a person is in the contemplative state: (1) ". . . we find no comfort in the things of God, and none also in created things." The second condition must be present or else we might attribute our "dryness" to self. (2) ". . . the memory dwells ordinarily upon God with a painful anxiety and carefulness, the soul thinks it is not serving God, but going backwards, because it is no longer conscious of any sweetness in the things of God." (3) ". . . inability to meditate and make reflections, and to excite the imagination, as before, notwithstanding all the efforts we may make. . . ." In the *Ascent of Mount Carmel* the saint gives three other signs, the first two of which are included in the third given above. However, his third sign in the *Ascent* is noteworthy: "The third sign is the most certain of the three, namely, when the soul delights to be alone, waiting lovingly on God, without any particular considerations, in interior peace, quiet, and repose, when the acts and exercises of the understanding, memory, and will, at least discursively — which is the going from one subject to another — have ceased; nothing remaining, except that knowledge and attention, general and loving, of which I have spoken, without the particular perception of aught else."[11]

Why must these signs be present before one is certain that he is in the contemplative state? The reason is that what they all indicate is the presence and operation of infused contemplation. Because of this gift the person experiences these phenomena; they are *caused*

[11] *The Mystical Doctrine of St. John of the Cross* (New York: Sheed & Ward, 1935), pp. 97–100, 35.

by the contemplation. The Holy Spirit is quietly leading the soul to apprehend God in a simple "grasp," if we may dare to use the term, in an unreasoned awareness. But this infused "light," this knowledge, is imperceptible at first. This is possible because it is not the product of the ordinary process of intellection — it is *given* to the intellect. The person's habitual prayer is no longer to be that which he and grace produce, but this new, passive, prayer. Hence, God withholds the grace for him to pray as he did formerly. Another explanation for his inability to use his intellect actively in prayer is that in infused contemplation — obscure and unknown as it may be — the intellect is already occupied, and cannot do two things at once. The person receives no consolation from the infused knowledge, which is "dry," with no effect on imagination and senses, therefore, with no ability to rouse the helpful emotions.

As a result, he feels that he is backsliding. Everything seems wrong with his prayer, and, in addition, temptations may be multiplied, disappointments and other trials may occur just at this time. But through it all he has a constant, single desire for God, burning, as it were, with a "cold" flame. God is his attraction, God in His simplicity, and for that reason he seeks solitude and God in that solitude, although, because of his inability to meditate and pray as he did formerly, the search is painful and confusing. The reason for his being drawn so strongly to God is that the obscure infused contemplation is exercising a powerful influence on his will. When God is so presented to his will, it is impossible for him to find comfort in anything less than God.[12] But he doesn't know all this. What he knows is that his spiritual life is "mixed up": he wants God alone, and yet he can't pray; his desire for God is much greater now than it was when he could pray with ease.

This condition is both what is known as the Prayer of Quiet — passive, not acquired — and the Dark Night of the Senses. St. John's advice is not to attempt meditation or our usual prayer but to maintain "a peaceful and loving attentiveness toward God,"[13] a silent co-operation with the loving knowledge infused in the intellect. The will should make no "acts," but simply possess and enjoy. But to keep the active intellect, which feels unoccupied, as well as the imagination, from wandering, it may be well to make a single, simple act, repeated and unreasoned, unnoticed, in fact, during the time of prayer.[14] The Prayer of Quiet admits of variations as well as degrees: the intellect becomes more or less aware of God's presence, grasped in this new mode; the awareness may be consoling or completely arid. But at base this prayer and state is characterized by the will being held by the infused knowledge, the other faculties feeling nothing. Although it is intermittent, the contemplative state has begun. There are spaces during which ordinary mental prayer is possi-

---

[12] Cf. Fr. Gabriel of St. Mary Magdalen, O.C.D., *The Spiritual Director* (Westminster: The Newman Press, 1951), pp. 49–51; *Mystical Doctrine*, p. 98.

[13] Peers, tr., op. cit., pp. 379–380.

[14] Cf. Chapman, *The Spiritual Letters of Dom John Chapman*, O.S.B., ed. by Roger Huddleston, O.S.B. (New York: Sheed and Ward, 1946), pp. 287–294, "Contemplative Prayer."

ble, and then one should return to it. More likely it will take the form of the prayer of simplicity, but one should always follow the dictum: Pray as you can.

This condition is also the Dark Night of the Senses. We have seen the effect of the initial infused contemplation upon the intellect and imagination. The imagination has nothing to do, and the intellect can perceive the divine knowledge faintly at best. There is no or little consolation in prayer and in one's relations with God. The person wants God, because the will sees the Good presented to it by the Holy Spirit, but without the correspondence of intellect and imagination this desire is "dry." Added to all of this, as we have mentioned, are possible temptations and difficulty in practicing virtue. Perhaps God may permit other trials, such as persecution. There are "breathing spells" when consolation returns and prayer is as it was before, but the ordinary state is the contemplative.

Apart from being the natural consequences of infused contemplation, the Night of the Senses is the result of God's purifying action. It is passive mortification, God taking us in hand and in His own way "killing" self. Our efforts, active mortification, while necessary, are not enough. God knows us better than we know ourselves. He must purge us of our attachment to consolations, try our charity, whether we love Him for Himself or His gifts, purge us of our pride, of everything in us that is opposing the process of being made into Christ.

There are higher stages in the contemplative state, well described by authentic contemplatives, e.g., SS.

Teresa and John of the Cross. There is the crucifying
Night of the Spirit, which prepares one for the highest
form of infused contemplation. But this is not the place
for a study of these. What we have attempted in this
brief description of the beginning of the contemplative
state was an indication of the possibilities of the life
of grace, the virtues and the gifts. Infused contemplation gives us knowledge of the divine nature of our
Head, knowledge of His being, of His Person of Son. It
gives us an intimate union with that Person. The Son,
in His divine Person, is the object of the Father's contemplation and love. He is the Person of the human
nature.

It is not the human nature which is our immediate
term, but God the Son, and we come to Him through
reliving His earthly life. Infused contemplation is God's
own way to create us in the image of the Person of
the Son. We must prepare and pray for it. And if He
bestows the grace of this likeness, we do not discard
the humanity of Christ: we see it as the Son sees it,
with His mind. Every detail will be precious, and infinitely valuable, and divine.

Although infused contemplation is entirely gratuitous
on God's part, we must pray and prepare for it, because
it is of itself the normal development of the supernatural gifts which the Father has given us through,
in, and with Christ. And when the Holy Spirit takes
us over, as it were, by means of this grace, there is
all the difference between performing a task with labored
difficulty and with great ease. We feel propelled, pow-
ered, to love God, and, in fact, we are, for in infused

contemplation we are mainly passive to God's action. Our activity consists in saying "yes" to everything He gives and asks of us. To prepare for this state of contemplation — this is the proper field for our activity: perfect fidelity to the infused virtues and the gifts and to all that these demand, especially to charity in all its forms (with the resultant detachment from self), humility, and recollection. We must seek God in all persons, places, and things, and go to Him in all.

But whether God gives us infused contemplation or not, we shall find that living by the gifts is, in St. Benedict's phrase, "to run in the way of God's commandments," that we become more and more driven by the mighty wind of Pentecost; the more attentive to the Holy Spirit and the more docile that we are to Him, the more are we impelled by His grace.

Let us keep our gaze on the risen Christ, who is the most concrete image that we have of God the Son. As He reached this glorified state through His suffering and working life, Passion and Death, we do also by our reliving the same life and Death. What characterizes the risen life is Christ's preoccupation with the Father: "the life that he lives, he lives unto God." We are the members of the risen Christ; therefore our goal is "alive to God in Christ Jesus"[15] ". . . that I may know him and the power of his resurrection."[16]

INDIVIDUAL PRACTICES

1. Have you "met" God? Has this gift been operative in your life?

---

[15] Rom. 6:10–11.   [16] Phil. 3:10.

2. Meditate on Christ, the Wisdom of the Father.

3. Ask God for the gift of infused contemplation.

4. Study its effects for the development of charity and zeal in the lives of contemplatives.

5. What are the dangers in disdaining it? of not going on when God gives it?

6. Meditate on the risen Christ and the "power of His Resurrection."

7. Meditate on Our Lady, Seat of Wisdom.

8. Make a synthesis of this book for yourself.

GROUP QUESTIONS AND ACTIVITIES

1. What is the relation between Christ as Wisdom and as Word?

2. Discuss: "Our forefathers kept on meditating and they got there just the same."

3. Discuss: "This contemplation is too much 'up in the clouds.' I want to 'keep my feet on the ground.'"

4. Discuss: "First the Liturgical Movement and now infused contemplation! Let's get back to the good old days."

5. Conduct a serious study of the infused Prayer of Quiet and the Dark Night of the Senses. What, when, how long?

6. May not many spiritual troubles really be the Dark Night?

7. Study the relation between infused contemplation and the apostolate in the life of a saint who received this grace, e.g., St. Teresa of Avila.

8. Make a study of the Rule and Constitutions insofar as they provide a favorable "climate" and preparation for the hoped-for grace of infused contemplation.

Suggested Books

I. HOLY SCRIPTURE

Bouyer, Louis, *The Meaning of Sacred Scripture* (Notre Dame: University of Notre Dame Press, 1958).

Cecilia, Sister M., O.S.B., *The Psalms in Modern Life* (Chicago: Henry Regnery Co., 1960).

Cerfaux, Lucien, *Christ in the Theology of St. Paul* (New York: Herder and Herder, 1959).

Guillet, Jacques, *Themes of the Bible* (Notre Dame: Fides Publishers Association, 1960).

Heinisch, Paul, *Theology of the Old Testament* (Collegeville: The Liturgical Press, 1955).

Kissane, Mons. Edward, *The Book of Psalms* (Westminster: The Newman Press, 1953), two volumes. Analysis and commentary.

McKenzie, John, S.J., *The Two-Edged Sword* (Milwaukee: The Bruce Publishing Co., 1956).

Moriarty, Frederick, S.J., *Introducing the Old Testament* (Milwaukee: The Bruce Publishing Co., 1960).

Murphy, Roland, O.Carm., *Seven Books of Wisdom* (Milwaukee: The Bruce Publishing Co., 1960). Excellent study of wisdom literature of the Old Testament.

New Testament Reading Guide (Collegeville: The Liturgical Press, 1960). Pamphlet commentaries on the books of the New Testament.

Wikenhauser, Alfred, *New Testament Introduction* (New York: Herder and Herder, 1958).

II. FATHERS OF THE CHURCH

Ancient Christian Writers (Westminster: The Newman Press various dates). Series of translations of individual Fathers.

Fathers of the Church (New York: Fathers of the Church, Inc., various dates). Same plan as the above.

Freemantle, Anne, *A Treasury of Early Christianity* (New York: The Viking Press, 1953).

Toal, M. F., ed., *The Sunday Sermons of the Great Fathers* (Chicago: Henry Regnery Co., 1958), three volumes.

Waddell, Helen, *The Desert Fathers* (Ann Arbor: University of Michigan Press, 1957). An anthology.

III. DOGMATIC THEOLOGY

Farrell, Walter, O.P., *A Companion to the Summa* (New York: Sheed and Ward, 1941), four volumes.

Putz, Louis, C.S.C., ed., *The Theology Library* (Notre Dame: Fides Publishers Association, various dates). A series translated from the French.

Smith, Canon George, ed., *The Teaching of the Catholic Church* (New York: The Macmillan Co., 1949). A reissue in two volumes of a series of monographs by English theologians.

Tanquerey, Adolphe, S.S., *Manual of Dogmatic Theology* (New York: Desclée Co., 1959), two volumes.

IV. LITURGY

Davis, Charles, *Liturgy and Doctrine* (New York: Sheed and Ward, 1960).

Jungmann, Joseph, S.J., *The Mass of the Roman Rite* (New York: Benziger Bros., 1959).

Marmion, Dom Columba, O.S.B., *Christ in His Mysteries* (St. Louis: B. Herder Book Co., 1939).

O'Shea, William, *The Worship of the Church* (Westminster: The Newman Press, 1958).

Parsch, Pius, *The Church's Year of Grace* (Collegeville: The Liturgical Press, various dates), five volumes.

V. SPIRITUAL THEOLOGY

DeGuibert, Joseph, S.J., *The Theology of the Spiritual Life* (New York: Sheed and Ward, 1953).

Tanquerey, Adolphe, S.S., *The Spiritual Life* (Westminster: The Newman Press, n.d.).

VI. RELIGIOUS LIFE

Carpentier, René, S.J., *Life in the City of God* (New York: Benziger Bros., 1959). Treatment of the vows.

Gleason, Robert, S.J., *To Live Is Christ* (New York: Sheed and Ward, 1961). Nature and grace in the religious life.

Marmion, Dom Columba, O.S.B., *Christ the Ideal of the Monk* (St. Louis: B. Herder Book Co., 1926).

Van Zeller, Dom Hubert, O.S.B., *The Yoke of Divine Love* (Springfield: Templegate, 1957).

Walsh, Bishop James E., M.M., *Maryknoll Spiritual Directory* (New York: Field Afar Press, 1947).

VII. VARIOUS TOPICS

Blosius, Ludovicus, *A Book of Spiritual Instruction* (London: Burns and Oates, 1955). A sixteenth-century classic.

Caussade, Jean-Pierre de, S.J., *Self-Abandonment to Divine Providence* (London: Burns, Oates and Washbourne, 1935).

Francis de Sales, St., *Introduction to the Devout Life* (Westminster: The Newman Press, 1956).

Gardeil, Père, O.P., *The Holy Spirit in Christian Life* (St. Louis: B. Herder Book Co., 1954).

Guerry, Most Rev. Émile, *In the Whole Christ* (New York: Society of St. Paul, 1959). Meditations on the Mystical Body.

Haley, Joseph, C.S.C., ed., *Apostolic Sanctity in the World* (Notre Dame: University of Notre Dame Press, 1957). For secular institutes.

Hock, Conrad, *The Four Temperaments* (Milwaukee: The Bruce Publishing Co., 1961).

Ignatius Loyola, St., *The Spiritual Exercises* (London: Burns, Oates and Washbourne, 1952). Contains the rules for discernment of spirits.

John Eudes, St., *The Kingdom of Jesus* (New York: P. J. Kenedy and Sons, 1946).

Lehodey, Dom Vital, O.C.S.O., *The Ways of Mental Prayer* (Dublin: M. H. Gill and Son, Ltd., 1951).

Lercaro, Cardinal, *Methods of Mental Prayer* (London: Burns and Oates, 1957).

Marmion, Don Columba, O.S.B., *Christ the Life of the Soul* (St. Louis: B. Herder Book Co., 1922).

Perrin, J. M., O.P., *Forward the Layman* (Westminster: The Newman Press, 1956). For secular institutes.

Philipon, M., O.P., *The Spiritual Doctrine of Sister Elizabeth of the Trinity* (Westminster: The Newman Press, 1948).

Vonier, Dom Anscar, O.S.B., *Collected Works* (Westminster: The Newman Press, n.d.), three volumes.

Index

(The only proper names indexed are those of founders of religious communities and secular institutes.)

279